# QUEER BOOKS

THE INSULTING PROPOSAL
(SEE "SIDE-WHISKERS AND SEDUCTION," PAGE 165)

# QUEER BOOKS

BY

EDMUND PEARSON

KENNIKAT PRESS
Port Washington, N. Y./London

QUEER BOOKS

Manufactured by Taylor Publishing Company     Dallas, Texas

ESSAY AND GENERAL LITERATURE INDEX REPRINT SERIES

DEDICATED
TO
THE LIBRARIANS
AT THE
NEW YORK PUBLIC LIBRARY

*Two or three of these chapters were written while
I had the privilege to be one of you. In
probably every chapter you have generously
given your help; as, every day, you are
helping the writers of many far
better—and a few worse—
books than this.*

E. P.

*New York
June, 1928*

# CONTENTS

vii

# LIST OF ILLUSTRATIONS

ix

# TEMPERANCE NOVELS

# QUEER BOOKS

## CHAPTER I

### TEMPERANCE NOVELS

D ID the temperance novels ever find many readers? I have been looking at a collection of two or three hundred of them, and the most striking thing about their appearance is their good state of preservation. I believe that any other battalion of fiction, less earnest and moral in purpose, would show more marks of service.

These books are from forty to seventy-five years old and while their backs show the effect of long decades of patience, as the dust settled on them, the gold lettering on their sides is as bright as ever. They have been drawn up in close formation on the shelves; not out skirmishing.

*The Crystal Fount,* a compilation edited by the most redoubtable of all temperance novelists, T. S. Arthur, was copyrighted in 1850. Its back, as it faces me on the shelf, is faded, and the red leather is peeling. But taking it down, the sides appear red and fresh, the ornate gold stamping looks as if new. The design of an elaborate fountain, spouting gallons of pure water, which is eagerly quaffed by naiads, tritons, and sea horses (who simply cannot get too much good water) indicates far less usage than that of many a profane novel not so completely devoted to teetotalism. It has been, for these seventy years, a holiday soldier, a stay-at-home, while the fighting has been done by the rough, rude, and intemperate.

The historian of "Gunga Din" pointed out that gin and beer were for men at Aldershot, but when it came to slaughter you would do your work on water. With books, however, it appears that the teetotallers stayed on the shelf.

It may be unfair to judge by single copies, and these originally from a private collection. Hundreds of different novels were certainly published, and I believe that with T. S. Arthur a first edition of twenty-five thousand copies was not unusual. Somebody paid to publish them, somebody bought them, and somehow they got worn out or lost.

My impression that they were seldom read is strengthened by the fact that almost the only one to have needed rebinding in all these hundreds upon which I have gazed is the only one with any real celebrity, the only one whose title the average person remembers: Arthur's *Ten Nights in a Bar-Room*. There was something about that name which preserved it in the memories of many who never saw the book. Parodists and wits played with it, but even the author never reached such heights again. He had tried, earlier, with the feeble *Six Nights with the Washingtonians* (i.e., the Washington Temperance Society) and twenty years later, in 1872, he again essayed frantically, with *Three Years in a Man-Trap*. But the first fine flavour was gone. His goblet of water had lost its sparkle.

The fact that *Ten Nights in a Bar-Room*, in its dramatic version by William W. Pratt, held the stage for many years had much to do with its familiarity as a title. Probably it is still being played somewhere, and played in all seriousness. It was revived—possibly in a scoffing spirit—in New York, in the spring of 1928, and ran for weeks.

The dreadful power of strong drink was never so thoroughly impressed upon me as when I sat, one afternoon, probably in the early '90's, and waited for the successive risings of the curtain, with its picture of the Bay of Naples, which separated us from the stage, in the Newburyport City Hall. As the grog shop was revealed in all its horrors we felt that dramatic realism was in our midst. When the drink-crazed father hurled the rum bottle into the *left wing*, the little daughter obediently trotted on from the *right*, exclaiming:

"Oh, Papa, you have killed me!"

Then she fell dead in the centre of the stage,

and we suspected, as I have often suspected since, that the Demon Rum does not always get fair treatment from his foes. We felt sure that not even a drunkard could pitch such a curve as that.

It is possible to suspect that temperance novels were chiefly used as gifts from good and reverend seniors to giddy youth. And that the latter, according to their docility, read them or left them alone. It would be a foul deed to say anything in mockery of the benevolent features of Timothy Shay Arthur. He was born, it is slightly ironical to note, in Newburgh, a town whose name afterwards came into celebrity for its association with a dish which had sherry for one of its most important ingredients. The list of his works fills columns of the catalogues; he founded a magazine, wrote histories, and very moral novels about married life —with recipes for its success.

But when you find that, in addition to dozens of temperance novels, he was the author of *Advice to Young Men on their Duties and Conduct of Life* and that he ventured to write advice to young ladies, as well, you begin to wonder whether the youth, even of the 1840's, '50's, and '60's were not inclined to take him in moderation—perhaps only in cases of illness or fatigue.

Stevenson, in his picture of Masterman Finsbury, in *The Wrong Box*, must have had a similar person in mind. For Masterman "would have

travelled thirty miles to address an infant school."
Few other writers were so industrious and so
ethical. There was Clara Louise Balfour, author
of *Confessions of a Decanter*, and a number of other
small books, hardly larger than tracts, and nearly
all published in London or Glasgow in the 1860's.

Mrs. Julia McNair Wright was given to jocular
titles, like *Jug—or Not* and *John and the Demijohn*.
Some passages in the latter, with their affectionate
descriptions of all kinds of old-fashioned dishes,
have made me wonder whether such books in the
United States to-day should not be held inflamma-
tory and be kept locked up.

Consider such paragraphs as this: "At Mrs.
Stafford's table, wine-sauce was plenty; tipsy cake,
wine syllabub, and wine puddings often appeared;
there was brandy in the mince pie, brandy cheese,
and brandy peaches; and on Christmas, following
roast pig and roast turkey, came a high dish of
lemon punch."

I shall not let many of my friends see this book;
it would move some of them to violence.

The villain on the stage, as Mr. J. K. Jerome
long ago remarked, is never allowed the gift of
humour. This is true, in the temperance novel,
of all who speak in defence of alcohol. Eloquence
and persuasion, irony and sarcasm are reserved for
the hero, for the good clergyman, or the reformed
shoemaker who is the local champion of total ab-

stinence. There are a few trifling exceptions. Mr. Stafford, in *John and the Demijohn*, bearded at his own table by his militant daughter Agatha, who demands that the pudding sauce be reformed, warns her against being "singular."

"I like to be thought singular; I positively enjoy it," said Agatha briskly.

Mr. Stafford is then permitted a faint touch of irony.

"Be as singular as you please," said he; "but not about my pudding. My depraved appetite demands the flavor of the apple whiskey."

And there is a moment of unusual tolerance at the climax of *Deacon Gibbs' Enemy*, by Mrs. A. K. Dunning. The Deacon is shown in the frontispiece, a fine figure of a man, resembling W. E. Gladstone. He stands with a stout cudgel amid the ruins of his wine cellar. He has seen the light at last, and is engaged in the holy work of destruction—with the result, admitted by the author, that the cellar is "filled with a rich fragrance," while the wine pours in a stream over the floor.

Mrs. Gibbs rushes in, before the Deacon has broken up all the bottles, crying:

"Hold! With us this has only worked harm, but even this wine may have a mission of mercy in the world. In some forms of illness it helps sustain sinking nature, and sometimes does good. It is a pity to waste it when it is so rare and costly."

The Deacon argues this a bit, but finally agrees to deliver the key of the cellar to his wife (we are not told who cleared up the wreckage) while she promises to open the door only to supply those who need the aid of stimulants "to prolong life or to modify suffering."

But rarely do they allow the Demon a leg to support him. I think that T. S. Arthur would have scorned the arguments of Mrs. Gibbs. In his work, *Strong Drink*, which purports to be a novel, Henry Pickering, for the offence of offering Amy Granger a glass of champagne at a party, has to listen to a lecture against wine, and in the end find his engagement with her broken off.

In the same book Judge Arbuckle ventures to challenge Dr. Gilbert's opinions on the subject, and is quite put to rout by a few well-selected words from the doctor, occupying nearly all of pages 322 to 352, or a couple of solid chapters. The doctor simply confounds him with arguments physiological, statistical, sociological. As a clincher, to make the judge's errors quite clear to the little social group who have gathered, the good physician makes a rapid diagnosis and points out to everybody that the use of wine has left the judge with a complication of diseases, among which cirrhosis of the liver and incipient paralysis are but the minor troubles.

That is what you got in one of Mr. Arthur's novels if you spoke up for even moderate drinking.

*The Mysterious Parchment; or, the Satanic License* was by the Rev. Joel Wakeman, pastor of the First Presbyterian Church of Almond, N. Y. The author records an epitaph which two worthies of the village wrote in pencil on the gravestone of the saloon keeper. Here are two of its gentle couplets:

"Almighty vengeance sternly waits to roll
Rivers of sulphur on your guilty soul;
Let hell receive him, riveted in chains,
Damned to the hottest focus of its flames."

This language, observes the Rev. Joel Wakeman, "appears" harsh and severe, but when one considers the offences of the dead saloon keeper, it is no more "than an enlightened philanthropy would dictate."

If this was Mr. Wakeman's notion of philanthropy, one would shrink from incurring his active dislike.

The titles of temperance novels are full of charm. Sometimes they seek alliteration's aid, as in *The Bar Rooms at Brantly* or in *The Rev. Dr. Willoughby and his Wine*. Others vary in their appeal; I am not concerned to read about *Dick Wilson, the Rumseller's Victim*, nor do I especially care what happened to *Minnie Hermon, the Landlord's Daughter*. But when I see *Isobel Jardine's History*, I wish to know what it was.

Rarely are they brief; *Cherry Bounce* and *The Crack Club* are almost alone in their brevity. The good, old-fashioned title and subtitle, duly punctuated with semi-colon and comma, in the manner of the dime novel, has the proper swing. You hardly need to look beyond the title page of *The First Glass of Wine; or, Clarence Mortimer.* To this group belongs Walt Whitman's temperance novel, *Franklin Evans; or, The Inebriate.*

There is a curious twist, reminiscent of Horatio Alger, in *The Little Peanut Merchant; or, Harvard's Aspirations.* And I feel that many a thirsty soul may trouble the repose of the second-hand book dealers to see if any practical information can be found in *Elsie Magoon: or, The Old Still-House in the Hollow.*

*Love's Eclipse*, by Clara Lee, is a contribution to *The Crystal Fount*, edited by Mr. Arthur. Mark Wilford is betrothed to sweet Marion Linvale, the gentlest, dearest, best-beloved in our pleasant village of Alderton. Mark, after a dissipated career in Boston, returns to Alderton, takes Marion out to drive, and has the audacity to stop at a wayside inn and order a bottle of pale sherry. It is an idyllic wayside inn, as one may see from the picture. He drinks three glasses of sherry and sings her one of Thomas Moore's songs.

Behold the dreadful result: a year later *Marion* has been laid to rest in the Alderton churchyard, while Mark, deeply grief-stricken, but apparently hale and hearty, stands sadly at her grave.

I admit that the moral escapes me; could Miss Lee have meant to suggest that a glass or two of sherry might have built up Marion's frail constitution, and did she slip this bit of diabolical propaganda past the editorial notice of T. S. Arthur?

It may seem strange that the novel was selected as the vehicle for these moral lessons. The author of *Mapleton*, Rev. Dr. Pharcellus Church, refers to that seeming difficulty, but strikes out boldly in defence.

"Those who brand every book of the kind as *a novel*, in an offensive sense," he says, "are at war with the constitution of our nature. . . . Instead of carping against light literature, it were better to charge it with truths and influences, purifying, profound and enduring, and send it abroad as a mission of love to mankind."

Dr. Church does his novel grave injustice when he calls it light literature. The message was sometimes sent abroad in verse. *The Mental Mirror, or Rumseller's Dream*, by J. Leander, is a poem more than two hundred pages long. The author begins with a stirring call:

"Rumseller, awake and arise from thy slumber!
 Behold the result that thy labor attends;
 Look forth from thy gorgeous chamber and notice
 Clouds rise from the pit where life's thoroughfare
    ends."

THE BOTTLE

SCENE 1st.—THE BOTTLE IS BROUGHT OUT FOR THE FIRST TIME: THE HUSBAND INDUCES HIS WIFE

THE BOTTLE

FROM T. S. ARTHUR'S *TEMPERANCE TALES; OR SIX NIGHTS WITH THE WASHINGTONIANS,* 1848

LOVE'S ECLIPSE
FROM *THE CRYSTAL FOUNT*, 1850

The second stanza invokes another foe:

"Awake from *thy* slumber! O moderate drinker;
No longer repose on thy soft silken bed."

Throughout this collection of books the "moderate drinker" is actually the principal villain, with the "rum-seller" and the drunkard as assistant imps. The authors merely disliked the sot, but they positively hated the moderate drinker. He was inconvenient to their arguments. The question why the rum-seller has a gorgeous chamber, while the moderate drinker is only allowed a soft silken bed, and whether such a bed is considered as the natural consequence of moderate drinking—these problems interest me, but leave me perplexed.

Extraordinary innocence is the characteristic of nearly all these novels, and as I have said, the descriptions of wines and of drinking scenes are almost loving. As the efforts, futile or not, of men and women who wished somehow to remove the evil of drunkenness, it is impossible to jeer at the authors, to deny them a certain respect, or to disagree with the truth of much that they said, however childishly, blatantly, or violently they said it.

They outraged nearly every artistic canon; they spoiled reams of good paper with the adventures of their puppet characters, whom they classified as bright angels or black fiends, according to whether they had "signed the pledge" or not. But for all this they can easily be forgiven; the more so since the temperance novel, with a rare exception, is as dead as John Barleycorn was supposed to be at the passage of the Volstead Act.

Cruelty to children, however, is one of the hardest sins to forgive, and the work of the writer of temperance tales for children came near to being unpardonable. Is it possible that anybody could wish to create with his pen such insufferable prigs or to hold them up as models? *Brave Boys and Girls*, edited by L. Penny, begins with

> "'Happy Johnny, how you grow.
> Do you chew tobacco?' 'No!
> And what is better yet,
> I never smoked a cigarette.'"

We may tolerate Johnny, but someone will certainly wish to lay hands on Little Alice, aged eight, who was taken sick, and, when very ill indeed, heard the doctor prescribe brandy for her. Looking up, she said as loudly as she could:

"No brandy for me; I'll die first! I'm a temperance girl."

We are left to suppose that she did die, so the story cannot be said to have an unhappy ending.

Then there is the story of Fritz and his badge. Fritz is a little German boy, "who lives not far from the wicked city of New York."

"Why do I call it wicked?" inquires the author. "Because so much whiskey is sold there."

This was written long before the days of national prohibition, and New York is held up to scorn, not for its new forms of law breaking, but merely because it was thought proper to teach children that cities are wicked and rural districts altogether virtuous.

Fritz joined the Band of Hope and wore his badge every day. Not long after, he was taken sick and had to stay in bed. But he insisted on wearing his badge, and had it pinned to his nightgown.

"Pretty soon his mother brought his medicine which the doctor had ordered—a glass of milk punch. Fritz protested, and said he could not take it, because he was a temperance boy. But his mother insisted, saying:

"'The doctor says you must take this if you want to get well.'

"'Well,' sighed Fritz, 'if I must take it, then take off my badge; I can't wear that while I drink it.'"

The genial immorality of this tale makes it fortunate that few children have access to such books. Perhaps one of the unexpected advantages of prohibition is that since there is no longer anywhere in the land any material for a milk punch, the tribe of Fritz, Johnny, and Alice must vanish, too.

MAKING THE EAGLE SCREAM

# CHAPTER II

## MAKING THE EAGLE SCREAM

TOM BAILEY, one of the four veritable boys in American fiction, spent an exciting Fourth of July, some time, I think, in the 1840's.

Few persons who remember the events of the day recall the fact that the Hon. Hezekiah Elkins, at one o'clock, mounted a platform in the middle of the square, and delivered an oration. To this, however, the Hon. Hezekiah's "feller-citizens" did not pay much attention, as they were too busy in dodging the firecrackers which were thrown among them by boys posted on neighbouring housetops.

In Missouri, in a village called "St. Petersburgh," another boy tried to celebrate his country's birthday. This boy was Tom Sawyer, and for him the Fourth of July was a failure. There was a downpour of rain, no procession, and the greatest man in the world (as Tom supposed), Mr. Benton, an actual United States Senator, proved an overwhelming disappointment, for he was not twenty-five feet high, nor anywhere near it.

That is all we are told about Tom Sawyer's Fourth, but I know perfectly well what Senator

Benton was doing there: rain or no rain, he delivered an oration, just as the Hon. Hezekiah Elkins did in Portsmouth, in spite of the bombardment of squibs. Neither fire nor water, heat nor gloom of night could stay an American statesman in the performance of this duty.

I have found Joel Barlow, author of *The Columbiad*, at it in Hartford as early as 1787, while there are extant at least four other Fourth of July speeches made on the same day, when this country was not yet in its 'teens. But 1800 was the time of great beginnings; from that year till 1876, the Independence Day orators worked so industriously that the thin pamphlets which preserve their eloquence are enough in number to fill a bookcase, while the dust that gathers on them is symbolical of their listeners' throats in those happy and thirsty days.

Sometimes it was a test for the aspiring young politician, sometimes a treat for the community, when a distinguished veteran chose to take the platform and call, in the usual manner, upon the Venerable Name of Washington, or set the soldiers of Valley Forge tramping again through the snows.

Not all these speakers prodded the American Eagle into raucous screams, nor did they invariably, in the course of the address, tear the azure robe of night and set the stars of glory there. At Hanover, New Hampshire, in 1800, the speaker was a junior

REVELRY UNRESTRAINED
FROM T. S. ARTHUR'S *DANGER; OR, WOUNDED IN THE HOUSE OF
A FRIEND*, 1875

TIMOTHY SHAY ARTHUR
AUTHOR OF *TEN NIGHTS IN A BAR-ROOM*

at Dartmouth College, and only eighteen years old, but as his name was Daniel Webster, it seems that the local committee were fairly perspicacious.

Edward Everett, Josiah Quincy, Richard H. Dana, John Quincy Adams, Charles Sumner, Caleb Cushing, Robert Y. Hayne—these were some of the distinguished men, who, at various times, acceded to the requests of the committees and favoured their audiences with an hour or two of polished rhetoric, which was certainly dignified, even if to-day it looks intolerably dull.

There is something about so much unrelieved oratory which makes us shudder; makes us wonder again if this nation is especially and viciously addicted to it. Such has been the charge. It is strangely significant to find, in Parkman's *Montcalm and Wolfe*, that nothing which North America had in the way of trials for these two brave spirits seems to have filled them with deeper melancholy than the dreadfully long speeches inflicted upon them by their Indian allies.

Is there something in the air or climate of the continent? It is absurd to suppose so; long-winded speech-making is not unknown across the Atlantic nor is bombastic oratory rare in Europe. But it is odd that the French and the English soldier each felt that he was undergoing a new and grievous form of torture as soon as he came to be entertained by the aboriginal Americans.

Anthony Trollope condescends to praise Emerson for a speech he heard delivered in Boston during the Civil War.

"To the national eagle," writes Trollope, "he did allude. 'Your American eagle,' he said, 'is very well. Protect it here and abroad. But beware of the American peacock.'"

In such speeches, Trollope continued, "Fluid compliments and high-flown native eulogium are expected. In this instance none were forthcoming."

And there are some wise reflections in James Bryce's *American Commonwealth*. Of the Fourth of July oratory he wrote, "The speaker feels bound to talk 'his very tallest.'"

He adds that buncombe had begun to subside by the time of the Civil War, and that the reaction towards simplicity was strengthened by the example of Abraham Lincoln.

The most dignified orator would seldom forego an allusion to current politics. During the period of 1800 to 1814, when some of the most alluring of these speeches were printed, the Emperor Napoleon, usually called "the tyrant Buonaparte," came in for various unfriendly remarks, and the occupant of the White House, if he was of the opposite party from the speaker, was described as a despot of similar breed.

This is conventional, and our boasted national sense of humour always halts hereabouts. There is usually some Senator or Representative in Congress to discover an intimate resemblance between the President and the Emperor Tiberius, or perhaps Tarquinius Superbus.

After the speech-making was done, there was a pleasant little interchange of compliment, which is often printed somewhere near the title page of the Fourth of July oration. Here is a specimen:

Douglass, July 5th, 1802.

At a meeting of a large number of Gentlemen of this, and the neighboring towns, convened to celebrate the anniversary of American Independence.

VOTED,—that the HON. BEZALEEL TAFT, AARON MARSH, BENJAMIN ADAMS, EZRA WOOD, jun. DAVID BATCHELLER, and the HON. SETH HASTINGS, Esqrs. be a committee to wait upon the REV. JOHN CRANE, and present him the thanks of this meeting for his spirited and patriotic ORATION, delivered by him this day, and request a copy of the same for the press.

BEZALEEL TAFT, Moderator.

Douglass, July 5th, 1802.

GENTLEMEN,

WITH your request I readily comply. I beg leave to add, that the honor, which you confer upon me, in the polite attention, you have now paid me, cannot fail of deeply interesting me in your happiness, and also in the prosperity of the large and respectable assembly who listened to the speaker, with decent and almost profound respect.

Gentlemen, I am your obliged
and most humble servant,
JOHN CRANE.

Mr. Crane's oration was given at Douglass on Monday, July 5th, and printed by Daniel Greenleaf at Worcester, Massachusetts, on the 16th. The printer, in liberal fashion, threw in the cut on the half-title page, not as a portrait of the speaker, but merely as an appropriate embellishment.

It will be noticed that the letters of the committee and the orator are dated the same day. In our time the compliments might have been summarily disposed of by telephone; at another time, later than 1805, an exchange of letters would have done it. In this instance, I prefer to believe that the Hon. Bezaleel Taft and the others did actually present themselves at the parsonage, with their resolution in hand; that the Rev. Mr. Crane thanked them, and begged to be allowed to retire to his study to prepare a suitable reply.

Then he added his wish that they await him in the dining room, where his Wife and Daughters would have the honour of offering them some refreshment—a bowl of cold rum punch. And that the Hon. Bezaleel, the Hon. Seth, and the others, did so await his return, and passed a pleasant and profitable quarter of an hour. After this, Mr. Crane rejoined them with his stately little note, reminded his wife that she had forgotten the plum cake, and sent his daughter, Dorcas, to fetch it.

Robert Y. Hayne was eminent enough in his day, but the place he occupies in American history is what is known in the variety theatre as the "straight man" or "feeder." Nobody knows what he said, on a certain famous occasion, but everyone knows what Daniel Webster said in reply.* In St. Phillip's Church, Charleston, South Carolina, on July 4, 1814, Mr. Hayne spoke to the '76 Association. Grandiloquent he was too:

"FELLOW CITIZENS!

"OUR COUNTRY at this moment exhibits one of the most interesting spectacles, the world has ever seen. A spectacle, so august, so splendid, so sublime, that it must be grateful to the sight of God and Man. Millions of freemen now crowd the temples of the Most High, and offer the incense of gratitude on his holy altars. Ten thousand voices, now chant 'A nation's Choral hymn for tyranny O'erthrown.' . . .

"In what then, my countrymen, does your supe-

---

*When this was first printed, a descendant of Senator Hayne informed me that it was my own withering ignorance if I did not know what the Senator said which brought forth Webster's "Reply to Hayne." The merchants of Boston thought so well of it that they had a copy printed on silk and forwarded to the South Carolina statesman.

rior lot consist? Does the verdure of your fields
delight the eye? The vineyards of France and of
Italy display equal beauty. Are your mountains
the objects of your admiration? Visit that unfortunate, though magnanimous people, who once like
ourselves triumphed over oppression, and in the
glaciers of Switzerland you will behold nature in all
her grandeur and simplicity. . . ."

In a few moments, however, he lets them into the
secret: "The United States of America is the only
free country on earth." Much may be forgiven
Mr. Hayne, however. We were at war when he
spoke, and the war was soon to take an unpleasant
turn with the capture of the city of Washington.

Four years earlier, on July 4th, in St. Michael's
Church in Charleston, one Hext M'Call addressed
the American Revolution Society. The printed
copy of his address which I have seen has been
annotated by a critic with a pencil.

"Let our harps resound the grateful theme,"
suggests Mr. M'Call, "let us bow at the altars of
religion and patriotism, and 'God, even our own
God, shall give us his blessing.'

"'Such honor, Ilion to her hero paid,
And peaceful slept the mighty Hector's shade.'"

But the critic is not pleased. He remarks, on the
margin of the page:

"Here is not a happy coincidence. Sacred and profane allusion ought not to be so immediately blended."

When Mr. Hext M'Call refers to the distance between America and Europe, remarking that the God of nature had destined us for the happy pursuits of peace "by separating us from the old continent by a wall three thousand miles thick," the gentleman with the pencil acidly observes: "not a very correct figure."

He relents at the sentence, "If we would be heard, we must speak from our cannon—if we would be felt, we must draw our swords!" This, says he, is "very fine."

But when the orator refers to the memory of Grotius and Vattel and says that: "The Hydra policy has arisen from their grave," the annotator suggests "its Den" in place of "their grave," and adds that it is "not fair to make this Hydra spring out of the graves of those great men."

And the most charitable of us must admit that the speaker was taking a liberty.

Sonorous were the words with which the Rev. Dr. Hooper Cumming greeted the assembled Firemen of New York in the Bowery Church, July 5, 1824.

"Auspicious Morn! which witnesses the noblest declaration that ever issued from the lips of patriotism. Auspicious morn! which gilded the manly brows, and dilated the benevolent bosoms, and strung the sturdy nerves of Jefferson, and Adams, and Franklin, and Sherman, and Livingston. Auspicious morn! which heard three millions of freemen exclaim, 'The sword of the Lord and of Washington.' Oh! it is good to be here. I congratulate you. I rejoice with you. I can without misgivings call you brethren."

Dr. Cumming's condescension was as magnificent as Pooh-Bah's. And although it is not apparent that the clouds of war were lowering, Dr. Cumming closed by an offer, in the case of invasion, to serve as chaplain for the embattled firemen, "a Bible in one hand, and a sword in the other."

The Fourth of July oration had aroused printed satire at least as early as 1859. In that year there was printed at Greenfield an "Address by General Herr Von Louis Kershoot, Poem by Jared Theophilus Sacksphellow, delivered before the Hardscrabble Yeomanry, July 4, 1859." It has the usual thanks of the committee, the request for the copy for the press, the orator's reply, and the speech and ode themselves—all in broad burlesque.

Rather better is *Mose Skinner's Centennial Book*, published in Boston in 1875 to anticipate the flood of rodomontade which was arising for the year 1876. The author writes:

"Any person who insinuates in the remotest de-

Doty reading his License. See page 116.

FROM REV. JOEL WAKEMAN'S *THE MYSTERIOUS PARCHMENT; OR,
THE SATANIC LICENSE,* 1857

THE CAR OF INTEMPERANCE
FROM *THE CRYSTAL FOUNT,* 1850

AN

# ORATION,

DELIVERED AT

DOUGLASS, *July 5th,* 1802.

gree that America isn't the biggest and best country in the world, and far ahead of every other country in everything, will be filled with gunpowder and touched off."

And Skinner's mock oration, given at "Bye-town," Vermont, in 1875, begins thus:

"Liberty-loving Patriots of this Great and Glorious Republic:

"One hundred years ago the spot where we now stand was located elsewhere. . . ."

In the year 1859, when the rhetoric of these orations was first satirized, there arose a speaker who far outshone all those who have ascended the platform on Independence Day and torn a passion to tatters.

Edwin H. Tenney, an attorney of Nashville, stands alone in his class. He dipped his brush deeper into earthquake and eclipse; he reached higher towards the starry firmament and dragged down more glittering orbs for his astonished spectators than all the Fourth of July orators who ever lived and breathed.

It was the 83rd anniversary of American Independence as celebrated at Rome, Tennessee. The Rev. Mr. King offered a prayer, and the Hon. Mr. Bains read the Declaration. There were speeches later in the day, by five or six other citizens (the Romans of Tennessee loved their oratory), but these evening speeches are not reported. This is fortunate, for anything which could have been said was anti-climax after Mr. Tenney had finished.

He opened with these words:

"Venerable, my Fellow Citizens, on the brilliant calendar of American Independence, is the day we celebrate. Venerable as the revolving epoch in our anniversaries of freedom is this avalanche of time. Venerable as the abacus on the citadel of greatness, thou well-spring of hope. Homestead of Liberty, we venerate thy habitation. Monument of immortality, we adore thy worth. Pharos of ages, we hail thy glimmerings 'mid the cataracts of life. Almanac of our country, we would utter thy welcome with reverent awe. Our towers and our battlements, our flags and our heroes, yea, garlanded navies, decorated armies, and unfettered eagles, sleepless at the approach of thy footsteps, have welcomed thee. The clap of thy welcome booms along tessellated lawns, frescoed arbors, and lipping rivulets; while the surges of eloquence join the music of freedom."

Borne upon his own surges of eloquence, Mr. Tenney took up the subject of the Revolutionary soldiers:

"Bleak as were their prospects, they enlisted for their country—desperation brooked their pains, for victory fed their agony—hunger they endured, for their religion was their liberty. Hammockless

and tattered—jaded and homeless—forbearing,
yet intrepid like soldiers, they accepted their fur-
loughs from eternity. Battalioned in gloom they
were pensioners for immortality. Circumspect in
design they were heroic in intrepidity. Schooled in
stratagem they were subtle in exigency—stately
in mien they awaited their destiny, and when
wounded and in agony the dew drops of death were
chasing each other o'er the insect's race-course—
shroudless and coffinless they are jammed in the
grave. Ravens croak their death knell and buzzards
chant their epitaph, yet the jargon of their eulogi-
ums cannot inumbrate their sepulchre. The worms
may have scattered as their bodies have frittered,
and earth hug the ashes of a tearless grave, yet the
recollections of ages will embalm their fidelity and
calify with benedictions each passing generation."

The Nashville lawyer was ahead of his time.
Sixty years later he would have won *The Dial's*
prize and been a leader in one of the schools of
literature temporarily patronized by Ezra Pound
or Gertrude Stein. Members of these schools would
have had no difficulty in understanding what Mr.
Tenney meant when he said:

"We must drop ourselves upon the pallid margin
of seventy-six, and emptied of prejudice lean upon
the gales freighted as they are with cargoes of
misery wet with tears from the battlements of
Canada to the batteries of Georgia. We must listen

to the floating wails and lamentations of orphans
and widows, of tories, and patriots, drifting through
our valleys all bloating with the gout of oriental
prostitution."

Gravestones and epitaphs had an appalling fascination for Mr. Tenney. He dwells upon the neglect
of sepulchral honours for the fathers of the Republic:

"Samuel Adams lies unmarked under a Boston
sidewalk. William Wirt has not a slab, though he
rests in the embrace of a grave-yard at Washington.
Baron Steuben is hid without a rock, yet it be-
speaks for New York a reckless posterity. If we go
to the heights of Abraham we look for General
Wolfe—but where? If we go to Kentucky we hunt
for the comrade of Washington, faithfulest, truest,
but not a willow to tell that John Champe was ever
there. If we return to New Hampshire and sit by
the remains of the hero of Bennington, we revert
with disdain, though not a worm now parades
around his desolated sepulchre. If we want to see
Ethan Allen, who did business for the 'great Jehovah and the Continental Congress,' we find a
mound of bulrushes and bullets is the last sad mem-
orial of Ticonderoga. Three of our Presidents lie
unhonored; but we will make but one more allusion to national neglect. Yet traitorous should we
be to the beatings of liberty should we gargle this
scene."

There are some subjects beyond his powers—as he sadly admits, when he says:

"We will not speak of Daniel Taylor, of his detection and stomach—of the emetic and bullet in whose periphery lay his passage to another world, yet the prodigality of opulence looms big o'er his grave. Wearying as is our tribute, we cannot pass without an allusion which must gladden the scene. To those veterans eulogy is preposterous and monuments unavailing, but a heart soaking with gratitude is never bleak nor serene. Cold calumny may chill it and life's icicles freeze it, but when thawed by recollections blood leaps through its veins. Could we learn from immortality their fame or presage their memory, the priceless league—the serried rank—the siren yell—the solemn march—the cracking bone—the flying flesh—the clinic pang—the grilling wail—the quenchless sigh and the clattering footsteps of that army welding sympathy to ages and liberty to life, will float like the dying groans of Calvary down the rapids of mortality, and whistling salvation among the whirlpool of nations, they will enter like their fathers a sea of bliss. We might pauperize our intellect, but we cannot dramatize their valor."

The orator speaks of the battlefields of the Revolution, and after referring to "Dorchester, with its blazing heights" which "now rattles through the welkin of admiring millions," suddenly demands of his audience: "Where is Valley Forge? Where is Saratoga?" Giving them no time to explain, he proceeds thus:

"All had head-quarters on earth, though many had for head-quarters the Almighty. With their knees as their minaret, and Christ as their Saviour, their deific peals stream along the jaded lines and flapping ensigns of the army, and touching the angelic wires with telegraphic flight, they dart through the labyrinths of other worlds to be printed in italics in the newspapers of eternity. Their message arrived and Jehovah answered it. That answer is on the parchment in yonder capital! He answered it at York Town and at Lexington, at Stony Point and at Trenton, at Concord and Bunker Hill. He answered it in the triumph of freedom over despotism, of truth over error, and he will remember at the judgment, for he will enroll the militia of America, in the orchestra of the universe.

"That day, Fellow Citizens, how ecstatic must be their jubilee. Were our intellect a volcano we would redden its lava and widen its mouth, as we contemplate the father of our country leaping from his grave and hailing the resurrection of his departed comrades—as we see the snowy forms, the lurid stare, the frantic yell, drifting towards the shades of Mount Vernon—as we watch the tensive heart, the telling look, the seraphic smile, crowding solicitude

with tears to play in the embrace of a Washington
—as we picture the once noble forms and shiny equipages of those now rued heroes gnawed with rust
and digested by insects, all polished for immortality
—as we view the martial step and prompt array of
battalions and cavalries marshaled by the drum-
sticks of another world, all eager for his inaugural—
as we listen to his last sad tribute to the land which
was the darling of his heart and septon of his bones,
so eloquent mid their departure—as we think of
them headed with the feathered ensign of America's
pride streaming through milky ways, and rain-bow
domes, for Jordan's banks, festive with cherubic
songs, and crowded with the boats of paradise, we
would fancy parades and serenades mid its roral
gales, lepid glens, and truttaceous charms, and all
ticketed for glory, and chartering immortality's
fleetest steamer, they muster the army—they un-
loosen the moorings—and pealing their last farewell from that hurricane deck, they start for Satan's
landing, and hearing from yon dismal cell Arnold
and his traitorous gang squirming mid the *vises
of retribution*, they foil hell's batteries and scale its
parapets, and doxologizing along the suburbs of
that aristocratic city, they join the deputation from
heaven's artillery, to be haled by the mayor in the
citadel."

By three o'clock in the afternoon, Mr. Tenney

had buried the last of the Revolutionary patriots and advanced to the Mexican War:

"We pay thus our dues to seventy-six; but we see in this assembly the Mexican soldier. You have a mortgage on our sympathies, for your cerebellum has been steeled at the bellows of liberty. This gray-headed flag, the genial proffer of a Carthage heart, once splendid and significant, wiping so often with the limber neck of its gentle bird, your chameleon forehead, stitched with glory, and hemmed with magnificence, eloquent with Webster's great sentiment, mid the stars and stripes that now flap the gales of a grateful country—Ah! its history from the old training day, now sorry with scars from bombshells, and bored with bullet holes, all redolent of victory, hued with blood from Palo Alto and Monterey, is your eulogy. Heroes of Tennessee! Champions of Mexico! That old silk flag—powder-burnt, shot-worn, its eagle sleeping, and its stars still twinkling, can you ask for a better eulogy?"

Current politics must have been fairly exciting in Tennessee, so shortly before the Civil War, but it is difficult to discover what the speaker thought about these questions. That some people were incurring his disapproval is evident in this passage:

"The inclemency of campaigns, the stubbornness of suffrage, with all the dynamics of its stratagem, racks the passions and churns the sensorium, slivering churches, and daggering families; and

THE FOURTH OF JULY ORATOR
FROM MOSE SKINNER'S *CENTENNIAL BOOK*

# AN

# ORATION,

## PRONOUNCED AT WILBRAHAM

## ON THE 4th OF JULY 1810.

### BY CALVIN PEPPER.

*Government is instituted for the common good; for the pro-
tection, safety, prosperity and happiness of the people; and
not for the profit, honor, or private interest of any one man,
family, or class of men :—*

Declaration of Rights.

## PALMER:

### FROM THE PRESS OF E. TERRY.

what is last but not least, theologians and theologasters quit the sinner's complaint and the costly Calvary to marry applause, to vent predilections, or perhaps destitute of material to bewail from pulpit or rostrum national wrongs and degeneracies, negligencies and indispensables, pulling the north from the south, picking flaws in our polity, piling maledictions upon necessities, bending myriads to sections, and almost saucing the Almighty, and all this for disunion; but darker, still more typhoid, and pitiable, they claim to be guardians of philanthropy, of souls and palates, of niggers and gin; they rant and sputter, scare credulity, alter affections, thrashing doubt and whipping prejudice, with reasons wrecked, fancies foundered, and Bibles ransacked—they lunge into society, mould the youth, tinker the heart, nurse the sceptic, ravish innocence, lamm the conservatist, woo the enthusiast, cementing every victory with prayers— handling the weapons of Calvary as commission merchants of Immortality—they hunt the sickroom, doctor the dying, analyze prospects, wheedle hope, and with liniments from Gethsemane ease and lenify an eternal plunge."

In this, however, he seems to range himself against those who were advocating secession:

"The two great problems of our duties and dangers and destiny as a republic, are before us, and its remedy or its corollary are ours. We may choose which we will, but religion and the Union, or irreligion and disunion, are the dilemma. The one, like the banyan tree, blossoms, re-roots and feeds us with figs, the other is as sober as the coffin and blacker than the tassels on the buggy of death. The one tells us to take the old route of conservatism, pay the pikeage and enjoy its solid bridges and levelled roads, the other to cut out to glory cross-lots, and run the risk of breechings breaking, and bogs, and rogues. The one tiring type lulls rancor, and heals gaps, sacrificing popularity and position to the great principles of the Union and demands our support; the other spurs malice and chafes revenge by broaching whims and churning doubts for converts."

Finally he admits, with a pessimism rare in these Independence Day orators, that the state of the Union was precarious.

"God was certainly with us then. He was with the first bullet that left the gun on the old dirt-road to Lexington. He has been with us in smoky and damp weather. He is with us now, but how feeble is his welcome; feeble, though we are jolting between spirituality and worldliness, dead broke— with fanatical trains and reckless conductors— feeble though at our peril, for tornadoes are ahead of us, and nothing but the artillery of Jesus full blast, with its steady aim and holy shot, can save us!"

We ought to know more about Mr. Tenney. Except that, a year earlier, he addressed the Young Men's Association at Great Bend, I have discovered nothing.*

What were this man's antecedents and history? Did he go to Congress, and if not, how could he have prevented it? Under whom did he study oratory? How did he get that way?

---

*He spoke on "The Romance of Reform." The speech is briefly quoted in Chapter VIII of this book.

# ALONZO AND MELISSA

# CHAPTER III

## ALONZO AND MELISSA

EIGHTY years ago, if a girl smuggled a book into her bedroom, to read in the silence of the night, to the throbbing of her own excited heart; or if a moonstruck young man carried a book with him to some solitary spot, it was fairly certain to be a copy of *Alonzo and Melissa; or, The Unfeeling Father.*

Three or four generations of Americans palpitated over this story. For fifty or sixty years, its pages were literally sprinkled with the tears of youths and maidens; its passages of ghostly horror chilled the blood of young boys and girls; while its pompous moralizings and supposed devotion to fact caused it to be accepted by the elderly and pious. It was a *true tale*, as its author rigorously insisted, and not a wicked, made-up novel; it could therefore be read without the moral ruin which followed the perusal of a fictitious story.

To-day, if you ask for it at a bookshop, you will be told, by nine dealers out of ten, that they have never heard of it nor its author. About fifty years ago it went out of favour and became known as a plug—an unsalable book. But for the sixty years before that it enjoyed a popularity and long life which few American novels have ever known. It is safe to predict that not one of the best-selling novels of this year will last one half so long or be reprinted half as many times.

From 1811, the year of its first appearance, it was printed and reprinted, issued and reissued, pirated by this publisher and that, north, south, east, and west. There were periods when a new edition of it seemed to come out every year, each time in a different city.

Its place of first appearance and its author are both disputed. The year is agreed upon by everybody. In 1811 there was published at Poughkeepsie a two-volume novel called *The Asylum; or Alonzo and Melissa, An American Tale, Founded on Fact*, by Isaac Mitchell. In the same year, at Plattsburg, N. Y. appeared *A Short Account of the Courtship of Alonzo & Melissa* . . . by Daniel Jackson, Jun.

It has been satisfactorily shown, so it seems to me, that *The Asylum* is the original work, and that the Plattsburg book is a briefer and probably pirated version. *The Asylum* is long and maundering; it contains two stories. Somebody—suspicion points to Daniel Jackson, Jun.—saw his chance; took an early version of the book—the story of the two lovers—and sent that down the ages, in one

volume, with his name on the title page. That is
the one which everybody read, and its story is
described here.

The adventures of the lovers were recalled with
amusement by Edward P. Mitchell, editor of *The
Sun*, in his *Memoirs*. A reader of the book, whom I
knew, was a lady who tried in her later years to
find a copy of it to show to her daughters as an
example of the kind of absurd sentimentality which
had once seemed to her impressive.

The author, in a brief preface, somewhat un-
necessarily expresses the belief that the story "is
not unfriendly to religion and to virtue" and that
it contains "no indecorous stimulants." He says
that it inculcates "a firm reliance on Providence,"
that it is not "filled with unmeaning and inexpli-
cated incidents . . . imperceptible to the understanding." "When anxieties have been excited by
involved and doubtful events," he says, "they are
afterwards elucidated by the consequences."

So they are, and so also, by this preface, is the
reader prepared to learn that the author placed a
firm reliance, not only on Providence, but on the
majestical sound of polysyllables.

Hoping that his descriptions of nature "will not
fail to interest the refined sensibilities of the
reader," the author begins his tale with admirable
directness.

At the time of the American Revolution there

were two young gentlemen of Connecticut—friends, and recent graduates of Yale College in New Haven. Their names were Edgar and Alonzo. Edgar was the son of a respectable farmer; Alonzo of an eminent merchant. Edgar "was designed for the desk"—we should say, the ministry—"Alonzo for the bar." They were allowed to amuse themselves during the summer following graduation, and did so "in travelling through some parts of the United States."

On one occasion Alonzo went so far afield as New London, where he met Edgar's sister, Melissa, who was then about sixteen.

"She was not what is esteemed a striking beauty, but her appearance was pleasingly interesting. Her figure was elegant; her aspect was attempered with a pensive mildness, which in her cheerful moments would light up into sprightliness and vivacity . . . . Her mind was adorned with those delicate graces which are the first ornaments of female excellence."

The hero and heroine met at a ball; someone presented Alonzo to Melissa, and the lady, so the author is careful to say, "received him with politeness."

"She was dressed in white, embroidered and spangled with rich silver lace; a silk girdle, enwrought and tasseled with gold, surrounded her waist; her hair was unadorned except by a wreath of artificial flowers, studded by a single diamond."

Alonzo was then about twenty-one.

"His appearance was manly, open and free. His eye indicated a nobleness of soul; although his aspect was tinged with melancholy, yet he was naturally cheerful. His disposition was of the romantic cast."

He is probably the first Yale man to appear in fiction, and it is remarkable, as Professor Reed has noted, that he is about the only one of them who is not a great athlete.

There was another person at the ball, however—Melissa's "partner"; the son of a gentleman of independent fortune in New London.

"He was a gay young man, aged about twenty-five. His address was easy, his manners rather voluptuous than refined; confident, but not ungraceful. He led the *ton* in fashionable circles; gave taste its zest, and was quite a favorite with the ladies generally. His name was Beauman."

We are not told from which college Beauman came. As he is plainly destined to be the rival of Alonzo of Yale, we might have suspected him to be a Harvard graduate. Nothing is said about this, however, and the reference to Beauman's voluptuous manners makes it practically certain that he was a Princeton man.

Nothing in particular happened at the ball, but a few days later, Alonzo, by a series of lucky chances, was able to take Melissa out alone for an evening walk. In the regrettable language of to-day they ditched Melissa's cousin and "his lady," and proceeded by themselves. It gave the author the first of his many occasions for scenic description.

"It was one of those beautiful evenings in the month of June, when nature in those parts of America is arrayed in her richest dress. They left the town and walked through fields adjoining the harbour—the moon shone in full lustre, her white beams trembling upon the glassy main, where skiffs and sails of various descriptions were passing and repassing. The shores of Long-Island and the other islands in the harbour, appeared dimly to float among the waves. The air was adorned with the fragrance of surrounding flowers: the sound of instrumental music wafted from the town, rendered sweeter by distance, while the whippoorwill's sprightly song echoed along the adjacent groves."

This is the first appearance in the book of the whippoorwill. This curious creature, which comparatively few people have heard, and still fewer have ever seen, does not really have a song especially adapted to moments of tender sentiment. It is nervous and fidgety rather than soothing. Still, it is to the credit of the author of *Alonzo and Melissa* that he did employ native birds, rather than follow the custom of some of our early writers, who ruthlessly imported English skylarks and Italian nightingales, in defiance of all probability.

If it were possible to interview the rival claimants to *Alonzo and Melissa*, Daniel Jackson and Isaac Mitchell, it would be easy to find out which was the author. Simply introduce the subject of whippoorwills and observe the result. The author of the work was hypped about them.

Here is the rest of the scene, as it presented itself to the young people:

"Far in the eastern horizon hung a pile of brazen clouds, which had passed from the north, over which, the crinkling red lightning momentarily darted, and at times, long peals of thunder were faintly heard. They walked to a point of the beach, where stood a large rock whose base was washed by every tide. On this rock they seated themselves, and enjoyed a while the splendours of the scene—the drapery of nature.

"'To this place,' said Melissa, 'have I taken many a solitary walk, on such an evening as this, and seated on this rock, have I experienced more pleasing sensations than I ever received in the most splendid ball-room.'"

The author adds:

"The idea impressed the mind of Alonzo; it was congenial with the feeling of his soul."

Evidently it impressed him so profoundly with its wisdom and beauty that it rendered him absolutely speechless.

It was clear to Melissa that she had said something so good that all further conversation was totally unnecessary and that she had better be content with the amazing success of her first remark. And so, although it is recorded that "They returned at a late hour," they maintained a complete silence for the rest of the evening.

If anybody thinks that this is intended to indicate that their lips were otherwise engaged, or that any such familiarities as kissing and holding of hands took place, then he knows little of the behaviour of the youthful heroes and heroines of the novel of this period. Doubtless, Alonzo proffered his arm to Melissa as they walked home together, but it is otherwise certain that as they sat on the rock together, a distance of not less than two and a half feet intervened between them, and that there was nothing in their conversation and conduct, even by so much as the fluttering of an eyelid, to suggest a flirtation.

In every detail, their carriage on that occasion was marked by as great decorum as would have been that of the Rev. Dr. Ezra Stiles, president of Yale College, taking a dish of tea with Mrs. Abigail Adams.

On the next day they all went home. Beauman

was there; he "handed Melissa into the carriage," and with some others travelled part of the way with them. But Alonzo and Melissa finished the journey alone. There was a brief visit with the father of Edgar and Melissa—a "plain Connecticut far- mer," who was rich, "destitute of literature," and a "rigid Presbyterian." Then Edgar departed for New York, to begin his studies of divinity, and Alonzo, in his native village, about twenty miles from Melissa's home, "entered the office of an eminent attorney."

He was much worried, however, about his in- ability to keep Beauman from dazzling Melissa with his attractions. One day, late in the summer, "he ordered his horse, and was in a short time at the seat of Melissa's father."

The young lady was sitting by the window when he entered the hall. She arose and received him with a smile.

"I have just been thinking of an evening's walk," said she, "but had no one to attend me, and you have come just in time to perform that office. I will order tea immediately, while you rest from the fatigues of your journey."

By the time they were ready to set out, there was some really remarkable weather, which has to be mentioned. As in the story of the fisherman and the enchanted flounder, in which the weather be- came more and more portentous each time the fisherman returned to the shore, so, as Alonzo and Melissa's passion became warmer, the weather adapted itself to the situation.

On this afternoon:

"A soft and silent shower had descended; a thousand transitory gems trembled upon the foliage glittering the western ray. A bright rainbow sat upon a southern cloud; the light gales whispered among the branches, agitated the young harvest to billowy motion, or waved the tops of the distant deep green forest with majestic grandeur. Floods, herds, and cottages were scattered over the variegated landscape."

This time the scenery provoked a more passionate conversation, and the author puts it into a form of dramatic dialogue. Melissa refers to the rock on the beach at New London, and says:

"'I know not how it happened; but you are the only person who ever attended me there.'

Alonzo: That is a little surprising.

Melissa: Why surprising?

Alonzo: Where was Beauman?

Melissa: Perhaps he was not fond of solitude. Besides he was not always my Beauman.

Alonzo: Sometimes.

Melissa: Yes, sometimes.

Alonzo: And now always.

Melissa: Not this evening.

Alonzo: He formally addresses you.

Melissa: Well.

Alonzo: And will soon claim the exclusive privilege so to do.

Melissa: That does not follow of course.

Alonzo: Of course, if his intentions are sincere, and the wishes of another should accord therewith.

Melissa: Who am I to understand by another?

Alonzo: Melissa. [A pause ensued.]

Melissa: See that ship, Alonzo, coming up the Sound; how she ploughs through the white foam, while the breezes flutter among the sails, varying with the beams of the sun.

Alonzo: Yes, it is almost down.

Melissa: What is almost down?

Alonzo: The sun. Was not you speaking of the sun, madam?

Melissa: Your mind is absent, Alonzo; I was speaking of yonder ship.

Alonzo: I beg pardon, madam. O yes—the ship—it—it bounds with rapid motion over the waves.

"A pause ensued. They walked leisurely around the hill, and moved toward home."

This torrid courtship continues for a few weeks, until at last Alonzo "taking her hand with anxiety" begs Melissa to deal with him candidly, and remarks that he will bow to her decision, as "Beauman or Alonzo must relinquish their pretensions."

Melissa, then "her cheeks suffused with a varying

glow, her lips pale, her voice tremulous, her eyes still cast down" utters this decorous speech:

"My parents have informed me that it is improper to receive the particular addresses of more than one. I am conscious of my inadvertency, and that the reproof is just. One therefore must be dismissed. But——"

And she hesitated, and once more "a considerable pause ensued."

They met again at the beginning of autumn, when—

"The withering forest began to shed its decaying foliage. . . . . The solemn herds lowed in monotonous sympathy. The autumnal insects in sympathetic wafting, plaintively predicted their approaching fate."

Still, however, everything hung fire, and Alonzo still addressed the lady as "madam." A few days later, Melissa's father, the rigid Presbyterian, announced to Alonzo and Beauman that on the morrow he would inform the two young men as to his daughter's choice. The whole face of nature, upon the evening of this fateful day, is dark with portent.

"The breeze's rustling wing was in the tree. The 'slitty sound' of the low murmuring brook, and the far-off water-fall, were faintly heard. The twinkling fire-fly arose from the surrounding verdure and illuminated the air with a thousand transient gleams. The mingling discordance of curs and watch-dogs echoed in the distant village, from whence the frequent lights darted their pale lustre thro' the gloom."

The whippoorwills, by this time, are treated practically like hired musicians: they "stationed themselves along the woody glens, the groves and rocky pastures, and sung a requiem to departed summer. A dark cloud was rising in the west, across whose gloomy front the vivid lightning bent its forky spires."

Next day, Melissa's father requested Alonzo and Beauman to withdraw with him to a private room, and as soon as they were all seated, the old gentleman "addressed them" in a speech one page in length. He maintained the suspense to the end, and at last announced that:

"I now inform you that she has decided in favor of—Alonzo."

Beauman was more or less broken up at this, but no trouble developed between the suitors. Indeed every precaution against an outbreak had been taken by Melissa's father, since one of the provisions of his speech had been that instantly upon its conclusion both of them should depart and absent themselves for at least two weeks "as it would be improper for my daughter to see either of you at present."

As if Alonzo had not had delay and vexation

enough, America and England took this inconvenient occasion to go to war: the "battle" of Lexington was followed by the battle of Bunker Hill*, and a "panic and general bustle took place in America." These things "were not calculated to impress the mind of Melissa with the most pleasing sensations."

The eminent attorney with whom Alonzo was studying received a commission in the American army and marched to the lines near Boston.

Alonzo thought that it might soon be his duty to "take the field," and he talked the matter over with Melissa. They "agreed to form the mystic union previous to any wide separation," and even picked out a village in which they might live after the troubles were past. It was a place chiefly inhabited by farmers, who were "mild, sociable, moral and diligent."

This village, which they called "The Asylum," a word with pleasanter associations than it has to-day, gave the name to Mitchell's novel.

"Here," said Alonzo, describing the prospect to his affianced wife, "will we pass our days in all that felicity of mind which the checquered scenes of life admit. In the spring we will rove among the flowers. In summer, we will gather strawberries in yonder fields, or whortleberries from the adjacent shrubbery. The breezes of fragrant morning and

---

*A romancer's license with the calendar, if these events are placed in the autumn!

A

SHORT ACCOUNT OF

THE

COURTSHIP OF

ALONZO & MELISSA:

SETTING FORTH THEIR

HARDSHIPS AND DIFFICULTIES,

CAUSED BY THE BARBARITY

OF AN UNFEELING FATHER.

In ev'ry vary'd posture, place and hour,
How widow'd ev'ry thought of ev'ry joy!...*Young.*

BY DANIEL JACKSON, Jr.

PLATTSBURGH, N. Y.

PRINTED FOR THE PROPRIETOR.

1811.

---

THE ASYLUM;

OR,

ALONZO AND MELISSA.

AN AMERICAN TALE

FOUNDED ON FACT

BY I. MITCHELL.

IN TWO VOLUMES.

VOL. I.

POUGHKEEPSIE:

PUBLISHED BY JOSEPH NELSON,

C. C. Adams and Co. Printer.

1811.

*He took her miniature from his bosom, he held it up, and earnestly
viewed it by the moon's pale ray.*

ALONZO IN THE CHURCHYARD
FRONTISPIECE TO *THE ASYLUM*

the sighs of the evening gale, will be mingled with the songs of the thousand various birds, which frequent the surrounding groves."

He did not particularize as to the birds, but we can be pretty sure which ones he had in mind.

Alonzo received a commission in a militia regiment, but was not yet ordered away. Besides, his father's affairs were causing anxiety. One evening the eminent merchant asked Alonzo "if it were not possible that his marriage with Melissa could be consummated within a few days."

"Alonzo, startled at so unexpected a question, replied, that such a proposal would be considered extraordinary, perhaps improper: besides, when Melissa had fixed the day, she mentioned that she had an uncle who lived near Charleston, in South Carolina, whose daughter was expected to pass the summer with Melissa, and was expected to arrive before the appointed day. It would, he said, be a delicate point for him to request her to anticipate the nuptials, unless he could give some urgent reasons for so doing."

Next morning, at breakfast, the agitated merchant addressed his family in a speech of two pages, in which he reviewed his financial career and condition, informing them that five of his ships had been seized in English harbours, as lawful prizes, and that, in point of fact, he was bankrupt.

At this moment, the sheriff and his officers came in and dragged the old gentleman off to prison.

This event had the most unfavourable effect upon Melissa's parent, the rigid Presbyterian, who now begins to emerge as the Unfeeling Father of the subtitle. The lovers had a gloomy interview, and as Melissa prepared to return from it, "a whippoorwill tuned its nightly song at a little distance." But the sound, "late so cheerful and sprightly, now passed heavily over their hearts"— the situation was becoming too serious for whippoorwills to be of any use.

Melissa's father now received his daughter's lover "with a distant and retiring bow," and introduced to him a new member of the family: an unpleasant comedy character in the person of a maiden aunt, who had "doubled her teens." This, as I understand it, meant that she was a haggard old crone of at least twenty-six.

The unfeeling father, in a speech of about a page and a half, told Alonzo that he must now relinquish "all pretensions to the hand of Melissa" —and immediately left the room.

The situation became worse and worse. Beauman, who had just come into a splendid fortune, once more appeared as a rival. Alonzo could only visit his love secretly by night, and converse with her from the garden, while she leaned out the window. Her father and the comic aunt had locked her in her room.

After one of these nocturnal interviews, Alonzo met Beauman, who was standing outside the garden wall. Beauman, awake to the requirements of the situation, immediately adopted the language of high romance.

"What, my chevalier," said he, "such an adept in the amorous science already? Hast thou then eluded the watchful eyes of Argus, and the vigilance of the dragon?"

But Alonzo quickly showed him that he had learned something equally as good at New Haven. Princeton had the ball but it was not yet in Yale's territory.

"Unfeeling and impertinent intruder!" he retorted, seizing hold of him, "is it not enough that an innocent daughter must endure a merciless parent's persecuting hand, but thou must add to her misery by thy disgusting interference!"

"Quit thy hold, Tarquin," said Beauman; "art thou determined, after storming the fortress, to murder the garrison?"

"Go," said Alonzo, quitting him;" "go, sir, you are unworthy of my anger. Pursue thy grovelling schemes."

Beauman then abandoned the manner of formal speech and returned to the customary conversa-

tional style, in a speech of two pages, ending with
the information that he was now going back to New
London. And that was all that happened that night.

Next morning Melissa is taken from home by
the comic aunt and immured in a Gothic castle or
dungeon, with a high wall and moat. It is rather
surprising to find this structure in Colonial Connecticut, but the aunt's explanation is that it was
built by Melissa's great-grandfather, as a fortress
against the Indians.

The fact is, of course, that the novelist, writing
shortly after 1800, and under the influence of *The
Mysteries of Udolpho* and the Gothic romance generally, was quite helpless. He could no more avoid
putting his heroine into a haunted castle, and sub-
jecting her to horrid groans and ghastly visions,
than the novelist of the present decade can escape
Freudian terminology and dreams of sexual
symbolism.

Soon, Melissa is having a terrible time. There are
footsteps and there are mysterious whisperings. An
icy hand grasps her arm when she is trying to go
to sleep. Voices call to her, and warn her to depart
—which, by this time, she would jolly well like to
do. An exceedingly unpleasant figure at last stands
at her bedside.

"Its appearance was tall and robust, wrapped in
a tattered white robe, spotted with blood. The hair
of its head was matted with clotted gore. A deep

**wound** appeared to have pierced its breast, from which fresh blood flowed down its garment. Its pale face was gashed and gory! its eyes fixed, glazed, and glaring:—its lips open, its teeth set, and in its hand was a bloody dagger."

More than twenty years ago a discussion of *Alonzo and Melissa* was revived in the literary reviews, and from all parts of the country elderly men and women wrote in to recall, with a glow of enthusiasm, the old attic in some farm-house in Connecticut, or New Hampshire or New York, where fifty or sixty years earlier they had undergone delightful chillings of the blood as they read this incident, which seems to us so crude.

For many of these youthful readers it was their first experience with a fictitious story; to them a full-blown novel was hitherto unknown. Many households had certain devotional books; perhaps Baxter's *Saints' Everlasting Rest* or Foxe's *Book of Martyrs*. But fiction, romance, tender sentiment, and ghostly adventure were represented for the first time by this story, and by it alone. Probably this accounts for the enormous success of the book, and for the new editions which kept coming out for sixty years.

To-day I could find only two copies, in a city which has millions of books, and the one through which I gained my first knowledge of the tale had been so worn at this point that pages were missing.

The book was rebound in such confusion that it was almost impossible to discern what Melissa did, or how she was rescued from her peril.

One fact was plain, however: Melissa was not easily stampeded. The horrendous figure vanished, leaving the room "involved in pitchy blackness." A "horrid hoarse voice" called "Begone! begone from this house!" The bed on which she lay then seemed to be agitated, "and directly she perceived some person crawling on its foot."

She sprang up, found the candle, lighted it, searched the room, and took the reasonable precaution of looking under the bed. But there was no explanation of the dreadful spectre or the other annoyances.

Next day, Alonzo got into the castle. He crossed the moat by a tree that fell during the storm which raged when the hauntings were at their worst. He rescued Melissa; but soon afterwards lost her once more. Every time he turned his back, some malign influence snatched her away.

Alonzo returned to New London, where he put up with a family named Wyllis—remarkable for being almost the only surname mentioned in the book. Here he fell ill of a fever, and had various other trying experiences, until, one day, he was finally crushed to the ground by reading in a paper this notice:

"Died, of a consumption, on the 26th ult. at

the seat of her uncle, Col. W. D——, near Charleston, South Carolina, whither she had repaired for her health, Miss Melissa D——, the amiable daughter of J—— D——, Esq. of . . . , Connecticut, in the eighteenth year of her age."

"The paper fell from the palsied hand—a sudden faintness came upon him—the room grew dark, he staggered, and fell senseless upon the floor."

There follow several pages describing Alonzo's delirium and ravings, his partial recovery, his solitary and melancholy days, and his final resolve to take part in the war. He offered himself to the captain of a warship at New London, and this officer, "pleased with his appearance," promptly made him commander of the marines. The hero's ill fortune was persistent. In the first engagement with an enemy ship, each vessel practically disabled the other, and while they were lying helpless, a large English frigate appeared, took captive the Americans, and carried them all to London.

Here Alonzo spends a gloomy time in prison. Beauman turns up there, sick and miserable, and after some affecting speeches, passes away. The author cannot contrive enough woes to lavish upon Alonzo, so he introduces, for an hour or two, a wretched young Englishman, who is in sorry plight in the same prison. He obligingly tells the story of *his* life, and the point of it is that his sister had

dressed up in a man's clothes and pretended to be a
rival for her brother's sweetheart. As a result of
this prank, he has murdered both the girls, and is
himself to be hanged next week.

After a bit, Alonzo escapes from prison, by making a rope out of his clothes. He lands on the streets
of London, at three in the morning, and stark naked.
He is more than a little dejected, and quite chilly,
since it is a very raw morning.

His first piece of luck, however, meets him in the
person of an English sailor, a midshipman on the
*Severn*, named Jack Brown. Alonzo confides in him,
making his whole situation known, and the noble
British tar takes pity upon his enemy in distress.
He clothes him, takes him home, and finally ships
him to France, with ten golden guineas in his pocket.
This lavish generosity is probably accounted for
by the fact that Jack is married, with four children,
and naturally has to have a great deal of money.

Like every other American in trouble in Paris,
Alonzo repairs instantly to the Embassy, and thus
we are admitted to the venerable presence of Dr.
Benjamin Franklin. He listens to Alonzo's story,
and with due regard for his own reputation as sage
and philosopher, sits in complete silence for fifteen
minutes. As a result of this deep thought he gets
Alonzo a job as clerk in a bookshop.

A few months later, Dr. Franklin calls Alonzo
once more to his house and tells him of his own

acquaintance with and indebtedness to Alonzo's father. He then delivers an eloquent and sonorous oration on life, death, and love, on the vanity of human wishes, on patriotism, duty, the character of the late Melissa, and Alonzo's obligation to return and help the struggling colonies.

He ships Alonzo back to America, and a few months later the young man is standing in the churchyard at Charleston, South Carolina, before a stone with this description:

Sacred
To the Memory of inestimable departed
Worth;
To unrivalled Excellence and Virtue.
Miss Melissa D——
Whose remains are deposited here, and whose ethereal parts became a seraph
October 26, 1776
in the 18th year of her age.

Alonzo's grief leads him to frantic demonstrations in the graveyard, and almost the only consolation he can find is that a nightingale is singing near by. Nightingales, the author explains in a footnote, are permissible in South Carolina. There is also a whippoorwill—"Melissa's favorite bird"—whistling near the portico of the church. (Some deception had been practised on this whippoorwill, as will presently appear.)

At a tavern, in Charleston, Alonzo becomes acquainted with a young officer, who gives him a great many hints about a mysterious young lady who wishes to meet him. There is much backing and filling, and great hesitation by Alonzo before he will so much as look at any "female." At last however, he calls upon her.

"She was dressed in sky-blue silk, embroidered with spangled lace; a gemmed tiara gathered her hair, from which was suspended a green veil, according to the mode . . . a silken girdle, with diamond clasp surrounded her waist."

After a little preliminary banter, the green veil was lifted by the young lady, disclosing the beauteous features of—Melissa!

In a moment—and for the first time in the book, so far as I can gather—she was in his arms. But the author had to make extended apologies for this lapse, and try to disarm those readers who might be horrified or annoyed.

"Sneer not, ye callous hearted insensibles, ye fastidious prudes, if we inform you that their tears fell in one intermingling shower, that their sighs wafted in one blended breeze."

The explanation of it all was that the deception had been necessary to foil the unfeeling father, the rigid Presbyterian, and keep him from marrying her to Beauman. The Melissa D—— whose death had been reported, the lady who was actually buried in the churchyard, was *another* Melissa D——, a cousin of our heroine. And near her grave, the whippoorwill was now whistling—led astray by false pretences, like the reader of the book.

They go back to Connecticut; the tyrannical father is mollified, and all the easier, since about this time Alonzo's father's ships come in, and he is once more restored to wealth. The "nuptials" are prepared.

"And now, reader of sensibility, indulge the pleasing sensation of thy bosom—for Alonzo and Melissa are MARRIED."

Accompanied by twenty men, with muskets and swords, they investigate the Gothic castle, and find that it is infested by "illicit traders," men who are carrying on contraband dealings with the enemy in New York City. These miscreants originated all the elaborate and expensive hocus-pocus to scare one girl out of the house.

They are always willing to go to enormous trouble to bring off their effects: the lineal descendants of these illicit traders now belong to an "international dope ring" which contrived ghostly business in five different crook dramas of the recent New York and London seasons.

By an odd coincidence, about the time of Alonzo's wedding, some English prisoners of war—sailors—are brought into port, and Alonzo finds his old benefactor, Jack Brown, deeply distressed and in manacles.

In a short time Jack has been exchanged, his

wounds healed, and he is sent home with a draft on London for £500. He returns to his wife and four children, and sets up a public house at the sign of *The Grateful American.*

Alonzo and Melissa are now in complete felicity, except that the bridegroom is called out now and then on militia duty, until the end of the war. They return to the village, which they had chosen for their original home. Here they build their cottage, prepared to enjoy all the charms of nature, which the author is ready to describe at the least provocation. All of those charms are present, and a new one—the strawberry bird—is introduced in the last paragraph. He comes in, however, as an addition, and not in substitution for their faithful accompanists, the whippoorwills.*

---

*Early American bibliographers give no help about the authorship of *Alonzo and Melissa.* The controversy is discussed, with a few references, in Dr. Lillie D. Loshe's *The Early American Novel.* I find, favouring Mitchell's priority of authorship, Professor Edward Bliss Reed of Yale, and Mr. Oscar Wegelin (private information). Practically convinced in favour of Mitchell are Dr. Loshe, and Professor Carl Van Doren in *The Cambridge History of American Literature.*

Favouring Jackson's claim are the late Sidney S. Rider (a militant Jacksonian) and the catalogues of the Library of Congress and The New York Public Library. Jackson's grandson also defends his grandfather's claim.

Those who vote for Jackson as the author apparently have not seen the final letter of Professor Reed, in the *Nation.* February 25, 1909. (The whole discussion was a very pretty quarrel, and it will reward the few hardy ones who may look it up.) Mr. Edmund Platt and Professor Reed found, in the *Political Barometer* of Poughkeepsie an earlier, serial publication of the story, in the version which Jackson used later. This serial publication was in 1804, when Jackson was *fourteen* years old.

Mitchell copyrighted the novel, but did not prosecute Jackson—perhaps for the reason that he died soon after its publication in book form; that is, in 1812.

# THE TRIBE OF GIFTED HOPKINS

# CHAPTER IV

## THE TRIBE OF GIFTED HOPKINS

Our young townsman, Mr. Gifted Hopkins has proved himself
worthy of the name he bears. His poetical effusions are equally
creditable to his head and his heart. . . . He is destined to make
a great sensation in the world of letters.
                                            —*The Guardian Angel.*

I T IS not hard to write mediocre poetry, or
poetry which descends from mediocre to something a little worse. Almost all of us try our
hands at it; we may have struggled painfully, but
on looking back and discovering how many others
were doing the same thing, with the same lack of
success, we see that the toil was not so great nor
the tragedy so poignant. Anybody can make a
drab failure of that nature.

To write a play which shall merely perish—fade
away from dramatic anæmia—is the common lot.
But to achieve one which is so brilliantly bad that
it can amuse audiences for years—this requires
unusual genius.

The similar gift in poetry is rare. Libraries are
full of poems which are certainly not good, nor very
bad, but merely uninteresting. There are thousands
of ambitious poets, over whose innocent or ludi-

crous verses their neighbours and townsfolk linger with unsympathetic giggles. But the number of them who have won more than local celebrity is small; perhaps they are fewer than the number of genuine poets of the first order of merit.

To become famous for queer poetry it is necessary to have a combination of unusual qualities. There must be an absolute inability to know what is ridiculous; absence of the sense of humour must be congenital. Great seriousness of purpose must exist, together with a persistent itch for literary fame. But all these will avail nothing, unless the poet has, in addition, a diabolical aptitude for the wrong word in the wrong place at the wrong time. Where many of us would stumble upon a passable phrase or thought, he goes unerringly to the incongruous and the absurd. He takes our breath away, and we wonder if he is fooling us. Such is the bard who is sealed of the Tribe of Gifted Hopkins.

There is "The Brave Page Boys," one of the hymns by Mrs. Julia A. Moore, the Sweet Singer of Michigan. The poetess describes the adventures of her heroes in the Civil War. Finally she comes to the youngest:

> "Enos Page the youngest brother—
> His age was fourteen years—
> Made five sons in one family
> Went from Grand Rapids, here.

VETERAN BLESSING HIS SON
FROM COOK'S *THE PLOUGHBOY*

The Ploughboy charmed his maid.

FROM COOK'S *THE PLOUGHBOY*

"In Eight Michigan Cavalry
    This boy he did enlist
His life was almost despaired of,
    On account of numerous fits."

Mark Twain had the rare gift of being able to
imitate the queer poets. His inspiration seems to
have been Mrs. Moore: he acknowledges this in
reference to his Ode to the Ornithorhyncus:

"Come forth from thy oozy couch,
    O Ornithorhyncus dear!"

with its remarkable fourth stanza, which rose to
heights beyond the power of the Michigan sybil:

"Come, Kangaroo, the good and true!
    Foreshortened as to legs,
And body tapered like a churn,
    And sack marsupial, i' fegs."*

In *Huckleberry Finn* he writes the "Ode to
Stephen Dowling Bots, Dec'd" which he attributes
to Emmeline Grangerford.

"And did young Stephen sicken,
    And did young Stephen die?
And did the sad hearts thicken,
    And did the mourners cry?

---

*In *Following the Equator*.

"No; such was not the fate of
  Young Stephen Dowling Bots,
Though sad hearts round him thickened,
  'Twas not from sickness shots.

"No whooping cough did rack his frame,
  Nor measles drear, with spots;
Not these impaired the sacred name
  Of Stephen Dowling Bots."

And in the description of the young Emmeline, her tastes, and literary methods, although it is in the language of Huck Finn, we can be sure that it is Mark Twain himself talking about poets of the school of Julia Moore:

"Buck said she could rattle off poetry like nothing. She didn't ever have to stop to think. He said she would slap down a line, and if she couldn't find anything to rhyme with it she would just scratch it out and slap down another one, and go ahead. She warn't particular; she could write about anything you choose to give her to write about just so it was sadful. Every time a man died, or a woman died, or a child died, she would be on hand with her 'tribute' before he was cold. She called them tributes. The neighbors said it was the doctor first, then Emmeline, then the undertaker—the undertaker never got in ahead of Emmeline but once, and then she hung fire on a rhyme for the dead person's name, which was Whistler. She warn't ever the same after that; she never complained, but she kind of pined away and did not live long."

Julia Moore differed from Emmeline Grangerford in that if she had slapped down a line and couldn't find anything to rhyme with it, she would *not* scratch it out, and slap down another. She would trust to assonance, or to nothing at all. But she was altogether in agreement with Emmeline in preferring themes that were sadful. The muse of each was distinctly mortuary: both ladies believed, with Shelley, that the sweetest songs are those that tell of saddest thought.

Mrs. Moore could write a stirring chant for a political campaign. Witness her "Hurrah for Cooper and Cary":

"Three cheers for Cooper and Cary
    Hurrah, boys, hurrah;
  Three cheers for our nation,
    In peace and in war;
  If it were not for our labouring men,
    What would our nation do—
  Take this in consideration."

But she was far happier when her themes were casualties; sudden deaths, and the fate of people who suffered fits. In her song of the "Ashtabula

Disaster" (to be sung to the air: "Gently Down the Stream of Time") she begins:

"Have you heard of the dreadful fate
Of Mr. P. P. Bliss and wife?
Of their death I will relate,
And also others lost their life."

The work of Bloodgood H. Cutter, author of *The Long Island Farmer's Poems*, suggests the query whether there may be some connection between an unusual name and peculiar skill in such verse. To support this, one could cite the South Carolina poet, J. Gordon Coogler, whose innocent ballads gave much amusement to the newspaper paragraphers in the '90's. Mr. Coogler's often-quoted couplet is almost the only survivor of his many verses:

"Poor South! Her books get fewer and fewer,
She was never much given to literature."

And the romantic work of Shepherd M. Dugger, *The Balsam Groves of the Grandfather Mountain* is in prose, to be sure, but it is an unusually poetic prose.

Mr. Bloodgood Cutter arose to fame by embarking on the *Quaker City* excursion together with Mark Twain. The Long Island Farmer poet bored his fellow traveller, and also patronized him:

"One droll person there was on board,
   The passengers called him 'Mark Twain',
He'd talk and write all sort of stuff,
   In his queer way, would it explain."

The queer poet, being an extremely serious person, always resents the presence of a humorist.

Much better than these, but still a curious figure among poets, is the author of *Attempts in Verse* by John Jones, "an Old Servant." The book is introduced, with an essay "on the lives and works of our uneducated poets," by the stately pen of Robert Southey, Esq., Poet Laureate.

Respect and humility can go no further than in the autobiographical sketch addressed by the Old Servant to Mr. Southey: he was writing not only to one above him in social station, but to the official leader of the singers of Britain. That John Jones could write verse of a certain naïve charm appears in the opening lines of his poem to a robin:

"Sweet social bird with breast of red,
   How prone's my heart to favour thee!
Thy look oblique, thy prying head,
   Thy gentle affability."

In spite of the odd names of Bloodgood Cutter, Gordon Coogler, and Shepherd Dugger, two of the most remarkable of this band of poets were distinguished in no such manner. Mrs. Moore, who was leader of them all, attained celebrity solely by her work. Another poet, astonishing enough in his way—and quite different from any of the others—had a name so commonplace that the task of unearthing information about him is complicated by that fact. He is, apparently, the least known of all: the Rev. William Cook of Salem.

Anybody who attempts to trace the William Cooks of this world through biographical dictionaries and genealogical registers finds himself in a maze. If they are not as the leaves of the forest, they are as the pages of Mr. Cook's numerous pamphlets. The makers of catalogues are reduced to differentiating these William Cooks as "the ex-Mormon," "the poultry-keeper," *et al.* Of the Salem poet, the patient folk who make the catalogue of the Library of Congress aver that he died in 1876, but as to when he was born, even they are baffled.

A friend of mine suggests that he is first mentioned in the second part of the *History of King Henry the Fourth*, when Justice Shallow commands:

"Some pigeons, Davy, a couple of short-legged hens, a joint of mutton, and any little tiny kickshaws, tell William cook."

Since this essay was first written, the poet has been made the subject of an investigation by Mr. Lawrence W. Jenkins, whose account of him is now in the *Proceedings of the American Antiquarian Society.*

*Volume 34, new series, Part 1.

Mr. Jenkins cites William Cook himself as authority for the statement that he was born in 1807. He studied at Andover, and at Yale and Trinity Colleges. It may be remarked, by the way, that in spite of his claim to the style of "Rev. William," Salem probably called him Billy Cook.

In a preface to one of his books, which I have seen, he speaks of "my father, the late Captain William Cook, a good man and much respected navigator," who "was duly appointed to reconnoitre the English fleet that appeared along the coast. The reader will learn how I daily assisted him and also the dates." I did not find the dates, but from this allusion it would appear that Mr. Cook was a veteran of the War of 1812. If he was born in 1807, he was engaged in patriotic service at a tender age.

He was, he says, "ordained in Christ's Church, Boston, by the late Rt. Rev. Alexander V. Griswold, D.D., the third day of May, 1837," and he has "officiated regularly in all 'good fidelity' to the gospel, in charity for all, who believe in our Lord, and avoid persecution."

He was an industrious writer, since he appears to have written and published more than forty books, or small pamphlets of poetry, like chapbooks. The period of his greatest activity was from about 1852 to 1874.

He had ideas of literary proprietorship, since a copyright notice appears in some of his books. He dabbled in Latin, Greek, Hebrew, and French. Of his literary theories he boldly and admirably says: "My rhythm is original and varied to please my taste."

He reverted to the custom of the ancient bards— he recited his poems in public.

"Invited by friends, ladies and gentlemen, I composed and read the poem, Chestnut Street. The First Canto was read in that Street, last June, at sun-set, the others a few weeks after that time. With cold fingers I sketched the designs of the illustrations when winter had a jubilee—the mercury in thermometers often sixteen degrees below zero— therefore no foliage is seen."

A small building which he erected on a hilltop was burned down. He had used this place for prayer and meditation, and believed that its destruction was intentional. In *The Result*, a prose sermon with occasional verses, he writes:

"While at home I preached this doctrine
Without any consent of mine
A being in destruction arch
Went to my Bethel with a torch."

The date of this outrage seems to be February 22, 1863. He has left record of at least two public addresses about education.

His books are remarkable; he is no rival to the Sweet Singer of Michigan in her peculiar field, but he is a far more interesting personality. He wrote, printed, illustrated, bound, and sold his own works.

I have no reason to suppose that he knew anything of William Blake; he resembled that great artist chiefly in that he was eccentric. But there is at least one illustration in Cook's long sacred poem, *The Neriah*, which, crude as it is, suggests that he might have seen and tried to imitate some of Blake's pictures. Most of his woodcuts, however, are of the order of those which are reproduced here. He made his own printing press, so I am told by Mr. George Francis Dow, "a simple lever contraption," and engraved his own wood blocks from which he printed his illustrations.

He sold his little paper-covered books at his home, or to the listeners who heard him recite in the open air. There are a number of his paintings in existence, and he did some work in crayon. Many of his illustrations which I have seen are amended in black lead pencil, while in one or two pictures he advanced from the "penny plain" to the "tuppence coloured."

The long poem, *Chestnut Street*, has five or six views in black and white of its rows of houses, and two other pictures partly executed in coloured crayon. One of them shows a maiden martyr, led to her fate by a soldier in Homeric costume—a scene which fails to suggest to my mind any  recollections of Chestnut Street, Salem.

William Cook was a man of honourable life, generally respected by his townsfolk, although laughed at by the young for his peculiarities. He was a familiar figure as he walked briskly along the streets of Salem in a soft hat and a dark blue cloak.

His belief that he was a poet, and his religious eccentricities, did not interfere with the fact that in other activities he was well balanced. He was successful as a teacher of arithmetic and book-keeping.

One of the crudest of Mr. Cook's pamphlets is his *Talk about Indians,* published in Salem in June, 1873. It is the seventh part of his work, *The Cor Felix*. The title page mentions that the Rev. William Cook, A. B., is also author of *The Eucleia —Ten Parts, The Neria—Four Parts, The Guides— Ten Parts*. The *Talk about Indians* is a dialogue between father and son:

> "Had those wild men strong oars
>     And sails—out-spread,
>   When by the storm-boat shores
>     They, joyous, sped?
>
> "No, but they paddles had
>     And skins of game,
>   For sails not very bad,
>     Were all the same.

"Now, Father, tell thy son,
    As Sailors food,
Could they not take the sun
    When so they would?

"Why no, my darling child,
    For work like that
They were too fierce and wild,
    Blind as a bat.

❋      ❋      ❋      ❋      ❋      ❋      ❋

"In such poor homes dwelt they,
    Hard was their lot,
Besides brush daubed with clay
    House there was not.

"Oh, their bad fire-places,
    We soon would choke,
And blacken our faces
    Amidst the smoke."

This pamphlet ends with a song:

INDIAN CORN

Corn, corn, sweet Indian corn,
    Greenly you grew long ago.
Indian fields well to adorn,
    ˙And to parch or grind hah ho!

Where shines the summer sun,
And plied his hoe or plough,
Blessing to men have you not gone
Making food of your dough?

Sing well, sing cheerly of corn-crop,
Good for bread or for pudding—
How gloriously white you pop
Let chime-praise-bells ring.

In England, in France and Germany
At morn, at eve, at noon.
Johnnie-cake and hommony
Increase the family boon.

An earlier poem, *The Ploughboy*, is dated 1854.
The opening stanzas:

"Low gable roof, and all sides brown
The cottage by the moor
Has a charming site out from town,
And the inmates were four.

"There Jerome and Roland were born,
And Ellen their sister,
Whose cradle rockers, so much worn,
Could be rocked no faster.

"Well Jerome, Roland and Ellen too,
    In their so humble life,
To love each other sweetly knew,
    Unused to noisy strife.


"Jerome they say had bright blue eyes
    As sister Ellen had,
And no neighbor ever denies
    Roland was a good lad.


"Their grandmother useful, though old,
    As people used to talk,
To those children good stories told
    At home or in a walk."


The rural picture is continued in the second part
of *The Ploughboy:*

"The moon poures all her charms to night
    On hill and plain around,
So friends come learn what rich delight
    Is with the Ploughboy found.


"Yes, come see his rural homestead,
    The farm and farmer's fare,
Where he for virtue was well bred,
    His parents' fondest care.

"Hark, hear that distant boo-oo-oo,
    As walking by moon light,
He whistles, instructing carlo
    To be still and not bite.

"Then coming round the woody hill,
    Among dark coppice shade,
In nocternal strains the whip-poor-will
    Gives him a serenade.

"His pony looks over the wall
    For his master's fond pat,
When he is at home, carlo and all
    Show their pleasure there-at.

"Th' wakeful turkeys loudly goble,
    Cows lick their hairy hides,
Each brute creature, as it is able,
    In his kindness confides."

Mr. Cook's favourite themes were religious, patriotic, moral, and romantic. He wrote *A Jubilant Canzonet for the Salem Infantry* and *The Martial Wreath Twined Respectfully for the Salem Independent Cadets*. But one of the events which stirred him most was that marriage which so caught the heart of America—General Frémont's with Miss Jessie Benton. He begins his poem "Fremont" in this wise:

### CANTO LATINUS

Nequis currit facile in sua vi,
    Libre proinde,
Vires dantur commodum eo rogantur;
    Ad bona car sit,
Canto juvat quemque gratis canere laudes,
    Itaque evax
Laete pro Fremonte et Jessie suscito carmen.

### THE CANTO TRANSLATED

No one in self with ease makes speed,
    Freely therefore
Aids are fitly granted where sought;
    If pious be th' heart,
Songs helps each one gladly to sing praises,
    So said 'tis huzza
Lively for Fremont and Jessie I make th' strain.

The Western scenes of the General's adventures
gave the poet an opportunity:

"Lo, yonder through the distant groves
    Th' raging buffaloes came
Rolling dust and bellowing sound
    Told that they were not fondly tame,

That they were not gentle as doves
As dashed the hunters through the droves
After game that hungry man loves,
And by the fierce daring combat,
Gained were sirloins juicy and fat.

\*     \*     \*     \*     \*

"Still were all things the camp around,
    In evening air clear,
On the outward point of high rock
    A bird was near the nestlings dear,
Think, my friends, if such scenes be found,
That Fremont in notes did resound,
Then Jessie in echo did bound,
Fremont though bold had a kind heart,
And that bird could move it like art.

"Now hush, while the bird sings again
    Fremont and Jessie,
Hark, as its voice again warbles,
    From the rocks echoes them bless ye.
As the bird, full of its wild strain,
Sings until its eyes naught plain;
Suppose such bird to sing were [?] fain,
To one's mind beloved friends to bring,
That bird might do a useful thing."

Billy Cook was born too early. Metre and rhyme
were often beyond his attainment, but in some of

POET FROM COOK'S *FREMONT*

FRONTISPIECE AND FIRST PAGE OF COOK'S *THE CHARIOT OF ISRAEL*

the modern magazines of poetry he could have dispensed with both. As for his pictures, if they should be exhibited to-day at the annual show of the Independent Artists, nothing could be said of them except that they obey conventional rules of design rather more, and are better drawn than fully one third of the works at that exhibition.

# THE UNFORTUNATE LOVERS

# CHAPTER V

## THE UNFORTUNATE LOVERS

AT THE age of eighteen, Mary Caroline Austin well deserved to be called an elegant female. Her anonymous biographer so describes her and makes it clear that Mary was the belle of her little village, in "the most romantic portion" of the State of Delaware.

Her father was a retired clergyman, a widower of advanced age and ample fortune. An Englishman by birth and a university man, he had "mixed much" with the aristocracy of Great Britain.

This mixing had given him a very haughty and aristocratic air, which did not escape the notice of the other villagers on the banks of the river Brandywine. However, they observed, he was a good man at heart, though undeniably proud and haughty. Alas, that a father's unbending pride——but, wait a bit.

The remarkable and deeply affecting narrative which relates the adventures of the Austins is concerned with events which took place in 1852, in the beautiful village of Mattawan, Delaware. The

facts are written by an eyewitness of the principal
scenes, and by Richard Austin, brother of Mary.
They may, therefore, be "relied upon as accurate
and true."

They may—by folk who believe that a horse-
chestnut carried in the pocket cures rheumatism,
and that unicorns become docile in presence of a
virgin. The pamphlet is one of those issued by
Arthur R. Orton, and all these solemn protestations
of truth are but his ingenious scheme for putting
over a novel, in days when many people were
taught that to write or read fictitious literature was
to set foot on the road towards hell fire.

Mary was in the perfection of her loveliness—
manifesting the most brilliant gifts of mind and
the most dazzling charm of person. Her dignified
and queenlike air impressed the spectator with a
sense of passion and of power yet undeveloped. Her
hair was black and glossy and richly abundant;
her eyes were bright and black, and looked so
laughing, so witty, and so deep and tender by turns
(writes our historian) that you could not but look at
them (as he rather tamely concludes) with the deep-
est interest.

She had attended the best female academies of
Philadelphia, Wilmington, and Baltimore; and had
received instruction from private tutors at home.
Her moral and religious training, under the care
of her aristocratic parent, was naturally unexcep-

tionable. Moreover, in the manner of heroines of the 1850's, she was a universal genius, and was equally famous for her skill in painting, music, singing, dancing, and other of the polite arts.

It will be unnecessary to say more when I add that her poetry (published in the Wilmington papers) was much admired, and was thought by many to be the production of the "Milford Bard," a celebrated poet in that State, now deceased.

So lovely a creature as Mary Caroline could not long "escape the attentions of young people of the other sex." In short, she had suitors, and this gave the Rev. Mr. Austin much anxiety. Whenever she returned from school, some gay young fellow from the city was sure to appear in the village for hunting or fishing.

This was as much a hollow pretence, as if the five and twenty Liberal Peers, and the five and twenty Conservative Peers, who in *Iolanthe* followed Phyllis to her village, had pretended that they came to shoot sparrows and angle for goldfish. These young men were seeking the heart and hand of the beautiful Mary Caroline—and seeking quite in vain.

That young lady had bestowed her affections upon the son of a neighbouring farmer, named Edgar Worthington. He, too, had been away at school, and had now returned (as you can see) a tall, handsome fellow, with a figure like a graceful

young Hercules, a brilliant complexion, bold, piercing eyes, splendid white teeth, and a delicate silken
moustache. The young people were already lovers;
fond, devoted, passionate lovers; they had told
their loves a hundred times; they had embraced and
sworn constancy.

Not, however, in the presence of the Rev. Mr.
Austin. That proud aristocrat thought that Edgar
was below his daughter in social station, and he was
as keen as mustard about social station. He drew
the trembling girl aside, one day, and asked her to
promise him that she would never wed without her
father's consent.

"Solemnly, and with God to witness your plighted
word," he added.

"I do! I do!" exclaimed the almost frantic Mary
Caroline.

The old gentleman then raised his daughter from
the floor, where she had fallen, in an Early Victorian swoon, and impressed a kiss upon her brow.
As he did so, she noticed that his lips were icy cold.

A few days later the distracted girl found that she
had been hasty in giving this pledge to her sire.
That reverend gentleman had called upon Edgar
Worthington in a formal manner, and requested
him to abstain from visiting his daughter. He further informed the young gallant that never would
he sanction a union between them.

"Mary!" cried Edgar, his voice throbbing with

emotion. "Is this true? Have you given such a promise to your father?"

"I have! Oh, fatal error." exclaimed the fond passionate girl, hiding her face against the broad chest of her lover.

From this memorable hour the lovers hastened rapidly and madly to their fate. They met clandestinely, and embraced each other more passionately than ever. Miss Austin was in a perfect chaos of love, religion, poetry, filial affection, pride, passion, fear, and almost revenge. Edgar was nearly as bad. He was the more excited by the presence in the village of some young swains from Baltimore, who not only called assiduously upon Mary Caroline, but seemed also (O, hateful thought), to meet the social requirements of that elderly aristocrat, her father.

Finally, Edgar could stand it no longer. He sent a note to Mary Caroline, asking her to meet him in a little grove near her father's residence, on the Sabbath morning, before the hour for church.

It was a calm and beautiful Sabbath morning; the air heavy with the odours of wild flowers, fragrant leaves, and buds, and eloquent with the songs of happy birds. The music of the Sabbath bells, from churches far and near, fell gently and sweetly upon the ear, as if mellowed by the very stillness and richness of the atmosphere.

Suddenly, a piercing shriek, the wild cry of a

female voice, rent the still air. The sound proceeded from the grove where Mary and Edgar were to meet.

The Rev. Mr. Austin was aroused by the cry, and so were a score of others. A crowd soon collected at the grove.

O horror! what a spectacle met their eyes!

There lay the lovely and accomplished Mary Caroline, her throat cut and gashed, and there, locked in her embrace, bathed in his own gore, lay Edgar Worthington!

The clergyman at first fell back aghast and then, seizing the body of his daughter and wrenching her from the grasp of the dying man, bore her rapidly toward his residence, shouting:

"Call a surgeon! Call a surgeon!"

When he reached the house, it was apparent that Mary Caroline was expiring. To his questions as to whether her lover had inflicted the fatal wound she answered by a sign: no.

To his further agonized inquiry whether this was her own dreadful deed, and if she were dying by a wound self-inflicted, she seemed to say "yes." Then she smiled sweetly upon the spectators and passed away.

Edgar Worthington's manly and genteel form had all this while been lying beneath the trees, surrounded by a small group of sympathizers. One of them bandaged his wounds, while others conveyed him to his father's dwelling place. Lower in the social scale than Mr. Austin, the father of Edgar did not have a residence, but merely a house.

Meanwhile, an appalling gloom surrounded the little hamlet; alarm pervaded the hearts of the village maidens; an awful sense of insecurity filled the minds of parents who had brave and lovely sons and daughters.

After many days, and under the tender care of surgeons, Edgar Worthington slowly regained his strength. As soon as he was practically well, he was securely shackled and put upon his trial for murder. He maintained that the awful tragedy was a double suicide; that Mary and he had agreed that, as they could not be happy in life, they would die together and seek another world; that the wounds were respectively self-inflicted, and that they had then embraced and lain down to die together.

The Rev. Mr. Austin, and his young son, Richard—who now appears upon the scene—were inclined to be bitter against Edgar. They scouted the notion of suicide, and pointed out that only one of the two razors found at the fatal tryst was stained with blood. This view seems to have been urged by the Government, and to have convinced the jury, for they brought in the unfortunate young man GUILTY OF MURDER in the first degree.

The author does not give a full account of the trial, but remarks that those who desire can get the report, published at the time, by order of the Court. (I'd like to see them do it.)

No sooner had. Edgar been condemned to death than a revulsion of feeling caused public sentiment to react in his favour. It was remarked that the Rev. Mr. Austin was an aristocratic Englishman, while Edgar was a handsome, noble-hearted young American, and moreover that if sympathy were to be lavished upon elderly fathers, what about old Mr. Worthington? A petition to the Governor for clemency was denied. This decision caused mutterings in the little Delaware village. Towards nightfall the jail was surrounded by masked men; the jailers were overpowered; the keys were seized; the condemned man was brought forth by friendly hands and driven away.

The Governor was now aroused; so were the officers; and so were the Rev. Mr. Austin, his son, and his friends. Some of these set off in pursuit. Thirty days later they had Edgar in gyves and manacles, leg bars and handcuffs, and once more in a dungeon cell, awaiting the dread engine of the law.

Among Edgar's visitors, during his last days, was a young surgeon from New York named Dr. Kelly. He passed many hours in the cell alone with the wretched convict, agreed to remain with him to the end, and, at the young man's special request, to take charge of his body after the execution.

Edgar Worthington behaved with the utmost

composure on the scaffold. He took part in the edi-
fying religious ceremonies, and was then asked if he
had anything to say.

He admitted that he would like to make a few remarks, and proceeded to speak: two pages full.

He reviewed his love affair with Mary Caroline,
and declared his innocence of any crime. He realized
that it was wrong to agree to commit suicide, but
that was the extent of his wrong-doing. He warned
young men and maidens against unrestrained
passion, and the elders against thwarting young
affections. He forgave his enemies and thanked his
friends, and asked that his body be given to his
kind friend, Dr. Kelly.

He shook hands all around, and was then duly
hanged, with all possible care; his body was turned
over to good Dr. Kelly; and, after a day or two,
buried by the sexton in the village churchyard.

One would naturally suppose that this was the
end of Edgar Worthington, and so, to all intents
and purposes, it might have been, had there not
returned to Delaware a few weeks later, one Captain Karsoll, who had been on his travels in Oregon.

This meddlesome old person solemnly declared
that near St. Joseph, Missouri, he had met Edgar.

Here was another excitement for the village. They
rushed to the graveyard; opened Edgar's grave;
exhumed and opened his coffin. In it was a log
of wood, shrouded in graveclothes, and with a wax

mask made to resemble the lover of Mary Caroline Austin. The family of that lady were now in a frenzy of rage, and Brother Richard soon set off to California in order to seek the murderer of his sister.

A year later Mr. Austin received a letter from Richard. It gave him great satisfaction and caused his aristocratic breast to swell with pride. He therefore passed it on to the newspapers, and thus we are privileged to read part of its contents.

"DEAR FATHER: I have a most extraordinary piece of intelligence to communicate to you. The story which Captain Karsoll told us about seeing Edgar Worthington near St. Joseph, was true. He did escape from the gallows alive, and came out to California. I could hear nothing of him here for many months; but three days ago I met him accidentally at the Clifton Diggins, from which I now write. He was in a drinking saloon, and was much intoxicated and delirious from the effects of liquor. I knew him at once, although he had evidently sought to disguise himself with heavy whiskers and moustache, green spectacles, &c. His face exhibited the most haggard and ghastly appearance, the effects no doubt of hardship, intemperance and disease. I knew him at a glance, but he did not appear to recognize me. I then spoke to him saying:

"'How are you, Edgar?'

"'The sound of my voice, calling that name, appeared to rouse him from his delirious condition, and he looked up, wild and trembling, and exclaimed,

"'Who are you? Who are you talking to?' using foul and profane epithets, which I shall not repeat. I replied coolly,

"'I am Richard Austin, whose sister you murdered, and you are Edgar Worthington, a fugitive from the gallows!'

"There was a crowd of people in the saloon, and they all started back with surprise and fear at this announcement. Edgar sprung into an attitude of defence, uttering a wild, demoniac yell, pulled off his slouched hat and a wig of false hair, revealing himself more fully to my view, and drawing a long hunting knife, exclaimed,

"'Yes, villain! I am Edgar Worthington! I did murder your sister, and I'll murder you for a song!'

"And he rushed fiercely towards me; but ere he had moved two feet I discharged my revolver, which I had drawn as soon as I saw him, and planted a bullet deeply in his chest. He fell, uttering the most horrible yells and imprecations; convulsions ensued, then delirium, and finally he sunk insensible on the floor of the saloon."

Edgar lingered, in great suffering, long enough to present a moral spectacle, and make a full confession. He acknowledged that the guilt of the death of Mary Caroline was chiefly his own; he proposed the double suicide and provided the razors.

"The manner of his escape from the gallows was extraordinary. He said that Dr. Kelly, the surgeon, was sent for by his friends to aid his escape. Dr. Kelly told him that if he could so fall as not to dislocate his neck or spine, he could save his life, and as Worthington was a strong muscular fellow, he thought he might do it. The neck, the surgeon said was seldom broken in athletic subjects by hanging, but they died by suffocation, by the air being shut out from the lungs. Dr. Kelly said that he had frequently opened the windpipe in cases of inflammation of the throat and in croup, and cases of suffocation by getting hard substances lodged in the air passage, and that the patient could easily live and breathe through a tube inserted in the windpipe below the seat of the difficulty. He thought he could operate upon the windpipe of the prisoner, and adjust a tube to the aperture, below the place where the rope would choke him, so that he could continue to breathe after he had fallen, if his spine should not be broken, until he was cut down, especially if the rope did not happen to obstruct the circulation of the blood in the great arteries and veins on both sides of the neck, as it rarely ever does. Dr. Kelly said he had studied this subject with great care, as one of the curiosities of science, and

# LOVE, SUICIDE, AND MURDER!

## THE TRUE HISTORY OF THE UNFORTUNATE LOVES

OF

# MARY CAROLINE AUSTIN,

AND

## Edgar Worthington,

PUBLISHED BY
ARTHUR R. ORTON,
BALTIMORE, PHILADELPHIA, NEW YORK & BUFFALO
1855

RAILWAY CAR SCENE, IMPROPER.

RAILWAY CAR SCENE, PROPER.

HOW TO BEHAVE IN PUBLIC
FROM PEALE'S *HOME LIBRARY*

had tried many experiments on animals to see if
the thing could be done, and he was satisfied, by
his course of study and experiment, that it was
perfectly feasible, and afforded a good chance of
escape.

"Worthington said he consented to try the
experiment, and the operation was performed in the
most skilful and ingenious manner. A small aperture was made in the windpipe, very far down,
below the upper line of the cravat, and a silver tube
was introduced, so contrived that it could be
covered, enabling him still to breathe through his
mouth, or uncovered, and thus breathe through
the tube alone. It was by no means a painful
operation, and was worn with much ease and com-
fort. He said he had much more difficulty in remov-
ing it and healing the wound than he had while the
tube remained there; and he exhibited the wound,
which was not yet healed.

"Everything worked as Dr. Kelly had predicted. The rope pressed only upon the right
arteries and veins, and left the circulation of the
other side somewhat free, although he was rendered
insensible by the pressure of blood upon the brain.
His neck was not broken by the fall, which you will
recollect was an unusually short one, and he
suffered very little injury from the attempt at
execution. He was cut down, by the kindness of the
Sheriff, before the usual time had elapsed, and

passed into the custody of Dr. Kelly, who immediately removed the body, applied stimulants internally and externally, and inflated his lungs artificially, and used other means of relief, such as bleeding, galvanism, &c, &c, and in two hours he was nearly as well as ever.

"A sham funeral was had, a watch set over the grave, and you know the rest. Worthington was got off in the night, and travelled by private carriage to Missouri, whence he started for California with a rough party and suffered all sorts of hardships, and much difficulty with his throat, having lost the dressings which Dr. Kelly had given him to heal it."

Finally, Edgar Worthington thanked young Austin for his kind services in shooting him, and then died—"peacefully and rational, with words of deep contrition and penitence upon his lips."

Richard returned to Mattawan, where he was gladly received by his reverend father. Not by the citizens, however, for the Austins had in some way become unpopular. So they moved away—to what place the author admits he does not know.

But he is sure that their story teaches a lesson of moral wisdom to every reader.

# GENTEEL BEHAVIOUR

## I

# CHAPTER VI

## GENTEEL BEHAVIOUR

### I

BIG books are published, almost every year, to inform us upon the latest rules of etiquette, or correct procedure in society. These are bought by the thousands, and consulted, it would appear, in secret. They give unfailing amusement to some of the writers of reviews, and are looked upon in mild derision by "the average man," who is content to think that if his behaviour is "rustic but hearty," then that's good enough for him.

In his opinion, such books are for women who give pink teas, or they may be read by contemptible men wearing pink spats. In any event, there is a degrading glow of pinkness about them and their lives.

It is true that in these enormous manuals of etiquette there are usually some pages which are faintly amusing. The author occasionally seems to be suffering agonies of the soul about forks, or letter paper, which are a little out of proportion in this Valley of the Shadow of Death.

In one guide to correct conduct, which I saw a few years ago, persons contemplating marriage were warned against "sensational ceremonies," as, for instance, having the wedding take place in a lion's cage or up in a balloon. It did seem to me that the number of people with these inclinations is almost negligible, and that the chance that they would, in any event, be influenced by the author's warning, is slight.

For the most part, the modern guides to etiquette are made up of definite information for those who wish it. And these people, as any bookseller can say, are very many in number. The humorist has to spend some hours to find anything ludicrous in these books—unless, of course, all etiquette is ludicrous.

That people will go to books for advice on almost any subject is one of the most touching of facts. If your pride of spirit does not forbid you to look at the card catalogue in a large library, go to the drawer marked "How" and see what is there to be seen. You may find two trays, filled to the limit with cards (much too well-thumbed) each one representing a book whose title begins with the word "How." They tell their readers How to do everything which the mind of man can conceive.

From "How to Raise Apricots" to "How to

Become Pope of Rome" (or almost as far) there are books of directions and advice on much more than you will ever need to know. The group of books on "How to Write Short Stories" used to be one of the largest, although it is not clear that the authors of any of these manuals had written any short stories of surpassing fame.

In the last few years, through the magazine advertisements, we have all become familiar with the surprising incidents in the life of a young man who is learning French by a simple method. By his proficiency he is able, every little while, to knock his friends absolutely cold. Although he has no great mastery of English, he can always relieve a difficult situation, by jumping into a rapid and idiomatic conversation in French with a visiting Vicomte.

There is also the morose man in evening dress, going sullenly home with his wife, in their car. She is furious with him for his conversational failure at the party. He mutters something about another fellow who had actually heard of Rupert Brooke. He wonders how this chap became so free with learning.

She explains it all. It was by reading a book—one single volume—which is the royal road to literary allusion and social charm. He buys that book, and at the next party somebody mentions the word "beauty." The man who was once so dumb in the

presence of wits and highbrows, instantly remarks:
"Is it not Keats who says that a thing of beauty
is a joy forever?"

And this makes such an impression upon a great
business man who is there—the president of a Nail
and Screw corporation—that next day he offers
the sparkling conversationalist the post of Assistant
District Sales Manager.

I find that these wondrous books were known to
our great-grandfathers. In London, as long ago as
1837, appeared the third edition of *A Dictionary* of
*Literary Conversation*, with some bright bits on a
great variety of subjects—all given in A B C order.
The book is dedicated to the Rev. David Williams
—a noble and holy gentleman, I am sure, for he is
described as the "Founder of the literary fund for
the relief of authors in distress."

The paragraphs are short, and frequently interesting, but the method of using the book is a puzzle.
Did you take it with you and keep it in your lap,
under the table, and then, if somebody mentioned
Apples, or Beëlzebub, or Catnip, hurriedly turn
to that page and mug up a few facts? Or did you
commit the whole book to memory before you
ventured out?

Whatever the procedure, you could find in it
something about Adam or Amphibiousness, Bal-
loons or Beards, Fanaticism or Fruit, Obscurity or

Organs, Rabelais or Royal Munificence, Valour or Virginity, War or Waxwork.

Suppose that somebody referred to Beards. It was decidedly soothing to be able to retort:

"All the ancient philosophers wore long beards."

If Superstitions were mentioned, the owner of the book was instantly ready with this contribution to the table talk:

"Formerly among the Romans, it was necessary to consult the appetites of the sacred pullets, before they elected a magistrate or went to battle."

The *Dictionary* had first aid for the tongue-tied, if the subject under discussion chanced to be Virginity. You had but to consult the book, look up, smile pleasantly, and announce:

"The virgins of Bologna amounted to the number of twenty, and they performed all kinds of needlework."

The guides to conversation are few compared with the books which are ready to teach the art of polite letter writing. These have almost always set up counsels of perfection; they seem to imagine a world that it is hard to believe could ever have existed. The author of *The Letter Writer's Own Book*, which came out in Philadelphia nearly eighty years ago, suggested this as an epistle to be sent:

### From a Young Lady in the Country to her Father, acquainting him with an Offer made to her of Marriage.

HONOURED FATHER,

My duty teaches me to acquaint you, that a gentleman of this town, whose name is Smith, and by business a linen-draper, has made some overtures to my cousin Arnold, in the way of courtship to me. My cousin has brought him once or twice into my company, as he has a high opinion of him and his circumstances. He has been set up three years, possesses a very good business, and lives in credit and fashion. He is about twenty-seven years old, and is likely in his person. He seems not to want sense nor manners, and is come of a good family. He has broken his mind to me, and boasts how well he can maintain me; but I assure you, sir, I have given him no encouragement, yet he resolves to persevere, and pretends extraordinary affection and esteem. I would not, sir, by any means, omit to acquaint you with the beginning of an affair, that would show a disobedience unworthy of your kind indulgence and affection. Pray give my humble duty to my honoured mother, love to my brother and sister, and respects to all friends.

I remain your ever dutiful daughter.

The father, I should add, disapproved of the linen-draper and forthwith commanded his daughter, whose name was Polly, to give him no encouragement at all. As Polly's love for Smith seemed to be so tepid, this parental command ought to have been easy to obey.

But if any father of to-day would be stricken, perhaps fatally, if he received such a letter as that from his daughter, what terrible suspicions would go through the mind of a parent who heard in this wise from his son at school:

*A young Gentleman's Letter to his Papa,*
*written from School.*

DEAR PAPA,

According to your Commands, when you left me at School, I hereby obey them; and not only inform you that I am well, but also that I am happy in being placed under the Tuition of so good a Master, who is the best natured Man in the World; and I am sure, was I inclinable to be an idle Boy, his Goodness to me would prompt me to be diligent at my Study, that I might please him: Besides, I see a great Difference made between those that are idle and those that are diligent; idle Boys being punished as they deserve, and diligent Boys being encouraged: But you know, Papa, that I always loved my Book; for you have often told me, if I intended ever to be a great

Man, I must learn to be a good Scholar, lest when
I am grown up, I should be a Laughing Stock or
Make Game to others, for my Ignorance: But I am
resolved to be a Scholar.

Pray give my Duty to my Mamma, and my Love
to my Sister.

I am, dear Papa,<br>
Your most dutiful Son.

That is a correct letter—and we cannot deny it
is a polite one—as advised by the author of *The
Complete Letter-Writer; or Polite English Secretary*,
which was published in London in 1792.

One other example, from the *The Letter Writer's
Own Book*, illustrates those peculiar situations
which, in the opinion of its author, are typical of
life's perplexities. Undoubtedly it may sometimes
be necessary to compose a note "From a Widow to
a Young Gentleman, rejecting his Suit." But this
Widow goes into so many details that to use her
model must require a great deal of snipping, cut-
ting, and pasting.

Here, however, is the way she did it:

SIR,

The objections I have to make to the proposal
contained in your letter are but few, but they demand some attention, and will, I believe, be rather
difficult to obviate.

You are, by your account, two and twenty. I

am, by mine, six and forty; you are too young to know the duties of a father. I have a son who is seventeen, and consequently too old to learn the duties of a son from one so little senior to himself. This much with respect to age. As to the little fortune I possess, I consider myself merely trustee for my children, and will not, therefore, impose on you by acceding to the common report, that I am rich. However, as you have borne a lieutenant's commission these three years, as you tell me, you may, perhaps, have reserved out of the profits of that, a sufficient sum to obviate every difficulty on that head.

I will press these objects no farther; when you can convince me that in point of age, fortune, and morals, you are such a person as I can, without reproach, take for a husband, and admit as a guardian to my children, I shall cease to think, as I now candidly confess I do, that motives far from honourable, or disinterested love, have influenced your application. Till that happens, I must regret that an ill-timed effort of gallantry, on your part, deprives me of the pleasure of subscribing myself

Your sincere friend and humble servant.

I think that the Young Gentleman was found out for what he was: a fortune hunter. Unless, in 1840, they paid a lieutenant far more than they did in 1918, the idea that he had "reserved out of the profits" of three years enough to "obviate every difficulty" would be greeted with unsympathetic cackles by a score of Young Gentlemen whom I once knew. At least, they were young ten years ago this autumn.

When the well-bred young man of 1792 received a proposal from a lady, and felt distressed about it, his first step was to write to a friend, as follows:

*To a Gentleman from his Friend, on a young Lady who had made him an Overture.*

I have just received a Letter, my dear James, which makes me the most unhappy of Mankind. 'Tis from a Lady whose Fortune is greatly above my most sanguine Hopes, and whose Merit and Tenderness deserve that Heart which I feel it is not in my Power to give her. The general Complacency of my Behaviour to the lovely Sex, and my having been accidently her Partner at two or three Balls, has deceived her into an Opinion that she is beloved by me; and she imagines she is only returning a Passion which her Superiority of Fortune has prevented my declaring. How much is she to be pitied! My Heart knows too well the Pangs of disappointed Love, not to feel most tenderly for the Sufferings of another, without the additional Motive to Compassion of being the undesigned Cause of those Sufferings, the severest of which human Nature is capable. I am embarrassed to the greatest

Degree, not what Resolution to take, which required not a Moment's Deliberation, but how to
soften the Stroke; and in what Manner, without
wounding her Delicacy, to decline an Offer which
she has not the least Doubt of my accepting with
all the eager Transport of timid Love, surprised by
unexpected Success. I have wrote to her, and I
think I shall send the Answer of which a Copy is
inclosed. Her Letter is already destroyed, but her
Name I conceal; for the Honour of a Lady is too
sacred to be trusted, even to the faithful Breast of
a Friend. I am,

Yours.

Next, he broke it to the lady in these delicate words:

*To a Lady, alluded to in the preceding.*

No Words, Madam, can express the Warmth of
my Gratitude for your generous Intentions in my
Favour, though my Ideas of Probity will not suffer
me to take Advantage of them. To rob a Gentleman, by whom I have been treated with the utmost
Hospitality, not only of his whole Fortune, but of
what is infinitely more valuable, a beloved and
amiable Daughter, is an Action utterly inconsistent
with those Sentiments of Honour which I have always cultivated. Even your Perfections, so strongly
are they rooted, cannot tempt me to be guilty
of breaking them. I must therefore absolutely

decline the Happiness you have had the Goodness
to permit me to hope for, and beg Leave to sub-
scribe myself, with the utmost Gratitude and the
most lively Esteem,

Madam,

Your most obliged

humble Servant,

J. THORPE.

These courtships seem so hopeless that it will be
a relief to hear of one that is successful, even though
it concerns a Person who is in Trade.

*From a young Tradesman to a Lady he had
seen in Public.*

MADAM,

Perhaps you will not be surprised to receive a
Letter from a Person who is unknown to you, when
you reflect how likely so charming a Face may be
to create Impertinence; and I persuade myself that
when you remember where you sat last Night at
the Play-House, you will not need to be told this
comes from the Person that was just before you.

In the first Place, Madam, I ask Pardon, for
the Liberty I then took of looking at you, and
for the greater Liberty I now take in writing to
you: But after this, I beg Leave to say that my
Thoughts are honorable, and to inform you who
I am; I shall not pretend to be any better. I keep
a Shop, Madam, in Henrietta-Street, and tho'

but two Years in Trade, I have tolerable Custom.
I do not doubt but it will encrease and I shall be
able to do something for a Family. If your Inclinations are not engaged, I should be very proud
of the Honour of waiting on you; and in the mean
Time if you please to desire any Friend to ask my
Character in the Neighborhood, I believe it will
not prejudice you against, Madam,

Your most humble Servant.

*From a Relation of the Lady, in Answer to the Above.*

SIR,

There has come into my Hands a Letter which
you wrote to Miss Maria Stebbing; she is a Relation of mine, and is a very good Girl; and I
dare say you will not think the worse of her in
consulting her Friends in such an Affair as that
you wrote about: Besides, a Woman could not
well answer such a Letter herself, unless it was with
a full Refusal, and that she would have been wrong
to have done until she knew something of the
Person that wrote it, as wrong as to have encouraged him.

You seem very sincere and open in your Designs; and as you gave Permission to enquire
about you among your Neighbours, I being her
nearest Friend, did that for her. I have heard a very
good Account of you; and from all that I see, you
may be very suitable for one another. She has some

Fortune, and I shall tell you farther, that she took Notice of you at the Play, and does not seem perfectly averse to seeing you in the Presence of

Your humble Servant,　　A. H.

Here is the young gentleman at school, again. This time he wishes to take dancing lessons, and overwhelms his papa with argument:

*From a young Gentleman to his Papa, desiring that he may learn to dance.*

DEAR PAPA,

Your affectionate and paternal Behaviour convinces me, that you are absolutely resolved to spare no Cost in any Branch of Education that is essentially necessary in the Employment you purpose I shall hereafter follow: And though I am certain you intend that Dancing shall have a Share in my Studies, nevertheless permit me to put you in mind of it, and also to desire you will no longer, on Account of the Strength of my Limbs, (which I am sensible is the Motive that retards me from beginning) delay your Orders to my Master; for I am persuaded, from an Instance, I am Witness of in our School, of a young Master, who is much weaker in his Limbs than ever I was, that dancing will rather strengthen than weaken my Joints.

It is not my Emulation for dancing a minuet, that is the Motive that induces me to be thus pressing; for, I presume, there are other Things more necessary belonging to this Qualification than that; such as to walk well; to make a Bow; how to come properly into a Room, and to go out of it; how to salute a Friend or Acquaintance in the Street, whether a Superior, Equal, or Inferior; and several other Points of Behaviour, which are more essential than dancing a Minuet.

These Points of Behaviour I often blush to be ignorant of; and have several Times been the Ridicule of those young Chaps, who are advanced in the Knowledge of this Accomplishment; And as I am persuaded you would not chuse I should be a Make-Game to any of my School-fellows, doubt not that you will send your immediate Orders for my beginning; which Favour, added to the many others you have already conferred, will greatly oblige,

> Dear Papa,
> Your most dutiful Son.

GENTEEL BEHAVIOUR

II

# CHAPTER VII

## GENTEEL BEHAVIOUR

### II

AMONG the books which aim to instruct in general etiquette, the reward is greater if we go back two centuries or more. It is true that in Mrs. Humphrey's *Manners for Girls*, printed in London only twenty years ago, there is a faint flavour of an era which seems already dead. Mrs. Humphrey warns that

"A nice girl is almost afraid to speak to curates, because she knows so well that most girls flirt with them."

This gives us a vision of the nice girl hurrying by the cage in which curates are exhibited, tossing in a bun, but refraining from conversation.

The same book remarks:

"A girl may have her name written ornamentally in some pretty tint across her note-paper, but . . . a stout, middle-aged woman, christened Elizabeth, does not do well to have 'Lily' written in pretty yellow ink across her notepaper."

This makes us feel that Mrs. Humphrey is, in her refined manner, understating the thing. To me, such conduct on the part of the stout, middle-aged woman, christened Elizabeth, has in it something like downright deceit.

One of the most influential books of etiquette was *Youth's Behaviour, or Decency in Conversation amongst Men. Composed in French by Grave persons for the use and benefit of their youth.* It was translated into English by Francis Hawkins (then eight years old!) about 1640.

It has recently been shown, by Mr. Charles Moore, that George Washington's famous "Rules of Civility" are taken directly from *Youth's Behaviour.* Someone selected and edited certain precepts from the book, and Washington, as a youth, copied them down.

The phraseology which seemed proper to Francis Hawkins had already become quaint when Washington's teacher adapted the rules, and in his version they have lost some of their Seventeenth Century vigour. Here are a few of the "General and mixt precepts as touching civility among men" as Master Hawkins turned them into English:

"In yawning, howl not, and thou shouldst abstain as much as thou canst to yawn, especially when thou speakest, for that shewest one to be weary, and that one little accounted of the company; but if thou beest constrained to yawn, by all means, for that time being, speak not, nor gape wide-mouthed, but shut thy mouth with thy hand, or with thy handkerchief if it be needful, readily turning thy face to another side.

"Hearing thy Master, or likewise the Preacher, wriggle not thyself as seeming unable to contain thyself within thy skin, making shew thyself to be the knowing and sufficient person to the misprice of others.

"Run not in the streets, also go not too slowly, nor with thy mouth open. Move not too and fro in walking, go not like a Ninny, nor hang thy hands downwards, shake not thy arms, kick not the earth with thy feet, throw not thy legs across here and there, and walking drail not thy feet after thee, truss not up thy breeches at every hand while, go not upon the top of thy toes, nor in a dancing fashion, nor in a stooping, nor in a capering, or in a tripping manner with thy heels.

"Being set at the Table scratch not thyself, and take thou heed as much as thou canst not to spit, cough, and to blow at thy nose; but if it be needful do dexterously without noise, turning thy face sideling.

"Take not thy repast like a glutton."

In 1720 there appeared an arbiter of taste in the person of Adam Petrie, a clergyman of the Church of Scotland. He was afterwards known as "The Scottish Chesterfield," since his success in teaching etiquette was apparently greater than his brilliancy as a preacher.

His *Rules of Good Deportment, or of Good Breeding* was followed by a set of rules for Church officers, and by "A Poem upon the Metaphor of Ministers being compared to Shepherds" which began with a line more pleasing to the ministers than to their congregations:

"O Faithful Shepherds of the Bleating Flock."

Petrie's book is rare, and has twice been reprinted in limited editions.* Like the others of this period it illustrates the wide variation between the extremely ceremonious courtly etiquette and the grossness of ordinary manners. Along with his counsels as to bowing and scraping, Petrie and his predecessors had to warn their readers from offences against common decency.

"When you give or receive any thing from your superior, be sure to pull off your Glove, and making a Shew of kissing your Hand, with a low Bow after you have done.

"If you be to travel in a Coach, let your Superior enter first; and when you enter, take the worst Place. The Hinder-end is the best; the right Hand of the Hinder-part is the first Place, the left Hand is the second Place, the Place over against the Person of Quality is the third, and his left Hand the fourth Place."

*Limited editions meant limited editions in the 1870's. Sixty copies or so; not the 2000 copies which some humorous modern publishers call a limited edition.

Of visits he says:

"Let your Visit be well tim'd, and, if to a great Person, see that it be short; and if he do you the Honour to wait upon you, you may say, *My Lord, if this great Honour be intended for me, it is beyond my Deserts.*

"It is yet more rude for any Man to rush in bluntly upon Women, without giving them time to appear with Advantage: They do not love to be surprised.

"It is rude and impudent to enter the House or Chamber of a great Person wrap'd up in a Cloak or big Coat, or with Boots or Whip, or with dirty Feet, or with your Gloves on your Hands. It is usual in many Courts that they deliver up their Gloves with their Sword before they enter the Court; because some have carried in Poison on their Gloves, and have conveyed the same to the Sovereign that Way. The Custom of having on the Gloves is not so nicely observed as formerly.

"If a young Man and young Woman be in a Room, and you be to remove from them, and if there be none with them, it is imprudent and un-civil to shut the Door after you; for if a person of a narrow Soul shall come and find them shut up in a Room, they may be ready to stain their Reputa-tion, which should be dear unto us, and cautiously preserved.

"It is unmannerly to scratch or make faces, rowl

your tongue in your Mouth, wink with your eyes, rub your hands, clack your fingers, shrug your Shoulders, look morosely, arrogantly or scornfully, to right your Garters or Buckles, or put off your Periwig, or comb your Head, or put off your Shoes or Boots, or appear in your Slippers or Night-gown, Cloak or Big Coat, before your Superior. . . . Smoak not a Pipe before Superiors, except they desire you. It is unmannerly to do it before Ladies, tho Inferiors.

"If his Lordship needs any Person, you must go and call him; but you must not bawl out his name on the Stairs or Window. . . .

"It is most uncivil and unneighbourly to hearken at People's Doors or Windows, or yet to peep in at them. 'Tis not only invading your Neighbour's Privacy, but is as much as if you broke open your Neighbour's House and riffled the same. It is both dangerous and undecent. Such deserve to be treated like thieves.

"If you have done any thing conjunctly with a Person of Quality, you must not say, *We did so and so;* you must only say in the singular Number, *His Lordship did so and so.*

"If an eminent Person plays on your Side, say not, *We have got the Game;* but *Your Lordship has got the Game.*

"It is not thought civil to write to a Person of Quality on common Paper, it should be on gilt

Paper, except the Person who writes be in mourning. . . ."

Petrie gives (with citations from Holy Writ) seventeen reasons against ingratitude; four against duelling, which he classes with murder; twelve against lying; about thirty against drunkenness; twenty against gluttony; and seventeen against adultery.

He advises against "promiscuous Dancing, obscene Songs, Stage-plays, Tragedies, Cards, Dice, Reading of profane Books." You could even be sinful, in Mr. Petrie's eyes, while drinking tea or chocolate. He writes:

"There is an irreligious and irregular Tipling of Coffee, Tea, and Chocolate. I call it *irreligious*, because I observe in Coffee-houses not one of a Hundred, either seeks a Blessing to it, as if it needed no Blessing; nor gives Thanks for it. . . ."

His chapter "Of Walking and Travelling" shows that he had studied Francis Hawkins's *Youth's Behaviour*, which later was to instruct Washington. Petrie's rules for conduct in the streets were:

"A Gentleman ought not to run or walk too fast in the Streets, lest he be suspected to be going a Message; nor ought his Pace to be too slow; nor must be take large Steps, nor too stiff and stately, nor lift his Legs too high, nor stamp hard on the Ground, neither must he swing his Arms backward and forward, nor must he carry his Knees too close, nor must he go wagging his Breech, nor with his Feet in a straight Line, but with the In-side of his Feet a little out, nor with his Eyes looking down, nor too much elevated, nor looking hither and thither, but with a sedate Countenance.

"When you walk with your Superior; let him have the right Hand; but if near a Wall let him be next to it. In *Scotland* the right Hand is only given, but in *England* they give the most eminent Person the Wall, and to all Ladies.

"When you walk with a Person of Quality keep not up to his Side, except he desire you; and when he speaks to you keep off your Hat. I do not mean here that Gentlemen of ancient and handsome Fortunes should do so.

"When you walk with Superiors you must not keep the Middle, but let the most eminent Person have it; and the next eminent Person his right Hand.

"Be sure not to walk with your Hands behind your Back, or in your Sides before your Superiors; nor must you handle any Part of your Body in their Presence."

Mr. Petrie thinks that the persons who believe it "rude to sit with their Back towards the Picture of an eminent Person" are over-nice. As "there are some rooms that are surrounded with such Pictures . . . there would be no sitting in them."

He is, however, at the top of his form when presented at Court:

"When a Sovereign allows you the Honour to kiss his Hand; at your first entering the Room into the King's View, you must make a low Bow, with a genteel Scrape with your right Foot, and then advance a little further, and do as above said, and so deliver with Grace what you are about to say; and after you have done, make your Obeisance with a humble Bow. It is like that the Courtier that introduced you will put his Majesty in mind, thus saying, *May your Majesty permit this Gentleman the Honour to kiss your Hand.* Then his Majesty will advance a little, and stretch out his Hand. You must then make a genteel Scrape, with a low Bow, quickly recovering yourself and advancing to his Majesty, and making a graceful Scrape with your right Foot, with a low Bow; and then fall down on your right Knee, putting your right Hand without your Glove gently under his, as it were to support the same; and after you have kissed his Hand, quickly recover yourself with a low Bow, as above said, and so retire a little Backwards, and wait his Commission. He may be addrest with some such Words as *GOD bless your Majesty, may you have a long and prosperous Reign, may your Dominions never want one of your Off-spring to sway the Sceptor over them.*"

Higher than this in stateliness the Scottish Chesterfield rises but once. He is a little hampered in the presence of God's Anointed, and can say but little. When, however, he announces his preferred formula for a proposal of marriage, he is able to indulge in some thoroughly genteel conversation:

"Madam, The many Perfections that do so illustriously shine in your Ladyship, hath so darted my Heart, that it is no longer in my Power to conceal my Affections from you, and to assure you that I am devoted to your Service. I should think myself happy if I should have the Honour to have Place in your Affections, and that you would look on my humble Service with favourable Reception, since I must own that my Love is centred in you above any Mortal."

"Sir, I cannot but own it my Honour to have such Room in your Affections, and esteem myself infinitely obliged to you for your kind and unmerited Sentiments, for which I return you hearty Thanks for your esteem of her who has not in her Power to give you Compensation, I being at the Disposal of my Parents, who only can determine that Affair; and I am willing to conform myself to their Pleasure."

The suitor then betakes himself to the lady's parents:

"Sir and Madam. With all Submission may I beg a Favour of you, who only have the Right to grant the same, that I may have Liberty of making my Addresses to your Daughter, whose virtuous

AN OVER-DRESSED FEMALE.

A NEATLY DRESSED LADY.

THE DUDE.

NEATLY DRESSED GENTLEMAN.

## HINTS ABOUT DRESS
IN PEALE'S *HOME LIBRARY OF USEFUL KNOWLEDGE*

FROM *THE LETTER-WRITER'S
OWN BOOK*

Charms and Accomplishments hath inspired me with secret Passion for her."

"Sir, Your gentleman-like Way of asking shows you to be a Person of Honour and Merit, which obliges us to yield to your Request. You may make bold with our House as often as you please. We wish you good Success; for we never design that her Affections should be chain'd to our Wills."

"Sir and Madam, You grace me with fresh Favours, for which I return you hearty thanks, and remain, Sir and Madam, your most humble and obedient Servant, leaving the Terms to our Parents."

"Sir, we also remain yours."

With this permission he returns to his lady-love.

"Madam, I have had the Honour of your Parents' Permission to make my Addresses to you."

"Sir, I cannot but with Pleasure behold you on such an Establishment, being sensible of your Affection, which (with Blushing) I must say hath kindled my Love to you."

"Madam, Be pleased to accept of this Ring, as a Pledge of my Fidelity to you."

"Sir, I accept of the same, and return you another, as a Hostage that I am yours. I have now thrown myself on your Protection, so that my Happiness and Welfare depends upon your Care, and the Tenderness I expect from you."

"Madam, Let there be no Delays of celebrating

the Nuptial Rites and Ceremony; I leave the Time to your Discretion."

One of the earlier books, and one to which the Rev. Mr. Petrie acknowledged his debt, was published in London in 1703. It was called *The Rules of Civility; or, The Maxims, of Genteel Behaviour, as they are practis'd and observ'd by Persons of Quality, upon several Occasions. Newly done out of the Twelfth Edition in French.* . . .

This book, perhaps more than any of the others, seems to have been intended for the guidance of the most obsequious of courtiers, and at the same time for the reform of outrageous barbarians.

An example of the one kind is given in the chapter which tells: "How we are to enter into the House of a Great Person: what is to be observed at the door and what in the Anti-Chamber."

Says the French author, under this heading:

"At the door of a Prince, Lord, or Great Person, it would be uncivil (if shut) to knock loud, or above one knock.

"At the door of his Chamber or Closet, it would be rude to knock; we are only to *scratch*. . . ."

And here is that rule of conduct toward portraits of great personages which Mr. Petrie deemed too exacting:

"Some have been so refined in Foreign parts, that they will neither be covered nor sit with their backs turn'd toward the Picture of an eminent Person."

Yet, in the same book, it was thought necessary to utter warnings like these:

"It is an unpardonable piece of Ill-breeding to make comparison with the Person to whom you are speaking, to discuss the Imperfection of another; as, to say, *I know such a Man very well, I have seen him drunk.*

"Or to tell a Lady: *I know her well; she is fat and swarthy, like your Ladyship.* Or to say before a Lady who is Flat-nosed, *It does not become such a Lady to pretend to be a Beauty, with her flat Nose.*"

When you visit a "Great Person":

"You must, when you sit down, observe to take a worse seat than his Lordship: a *Chair with Arms is the best;* a *back Chair* is the next; and a *Stool* the worst of the three."

What you should do if his Lordship should be so abandoned as to choose a Stool to sit upon, I cannot imagine. Probably you must then wallow upon the floor.

It was needful, according to the author of *The Rules of Civility* to remind his readers that:

"It is not becoming a Person of quality, when in the Company of Ladies, to handle them roughly; to put his hand in their necks, or bosoms; to kiss them by surprize; to tear their Fans; to snatch away their Hankerchiefs; to rob them of their Ribbands, and put them into his Hat; to force their Letters or Books from them; to look into their

Papers, &c. You must be very familiar to use them at that rate: and unless you be so, nothing can be more indecent, or render you more odious."

Let us suppose that you are actually in conversation with, or even near, a Great Person. You have removed your hat, but have been graciously commanded to put it on again. There is, let us say, a driving snow-storm. Here is the author's suggestion for your conduct:

"The Person of Quality having oblig'd you to be cover'd in a place where you ought not to have done it but by particular Command, you must pull off your Hat as often as in the Discourse his Lordship's name is mention'd, the name of any of his Relatives, or of any Person of Quality, that is intimate with him."

This is too much for the English translator, who adds a note, saying:

"This Precept is altogether unnecessary, and never to be practis'd."

And even the French author realizes that all this covering and uncovering may become absurd, for he writes:

"But if they happen to be nam'd so often, that your Civility becomes troublesome, you may desist upon the least encouragement from his Lordship."

There is a section to tell readers how they should comport themselves at church. The cautious translator advises:

"This book being written by a Papist, for Persons of his Perswasion, a Protestant ought to read this chapter with Caution, and with some grains of Allowance to the Author's Religion."

I am unable to detect anything especially Papistical in the chapter. The most protesting Protestant can surely agree to such a rule as this:

"It is undecent to comb your Head, or mend any thing about your Cloaths in the Church; to do which, if there be a necessity, you must take your opportunity and go out."

When dinner-time arrives:

"'Tis not manners, as soon as you are sit at the table to bawl out, *I eat none of this, I eat none of that; I care for no Rabbit; I love nothing that tasts of Pepper, Nutmeg, Onions, etc.*"

However much doffing of the hat was commanded before a Great Person, the Rules did acknowledge our natural human weaknesses. In eating:—

"If you happen to burn your Mouth, you must endure it if possible; if not, you must convey what you have in your Mouth privately upon your Plate, and give it away to the Footman: For tho' Civility obliges you to be neat, there is no necessity you should burn out your Guts."

This author is always at his best when he tells us how to behave before his Lordship, and to the sections about conduct with a Person of Quality, I return with unfailing pleasure. How useful it is, and how needful, to be reminded that:

"In Conference with a Person of Quality, it would be sawcy and ridiculous to pull him by the Buttons, the Sleeve, or the Hand, and most of all, to punch him on the Stomach."

CROTCHETS

# CHAPTER VIII

## CROTCHETS

RARELY, nowadays, can anyone devise a startling title for a book. All the surprises and sensations have been tried. The author has to shout pretty loud or else use a big big Damn.

A few years ago, a writer did exactly this, and produced a large and impressive book, whose title made everyone jump.

The contents were readable; there was evidence of great industry, and some indications of scholarship. It did not seem to be the work of a crank.

Yet when one came to discover what it was all about—and this required patience—the result showed that the author could not easily get a post as teacher in any scientific institute. For its theme was this:

Great numbers of strange objects—usually called meteorites—have fallen on the earth throughout the centuries. (The author compiled an enormous list of them.) These are supposed to be the results of celestial accidents: to be fragments of exploded comets or asteroids. But this theory is entirely wrong. These objects are weapons, thrown with mischievous intent at the inhabitants of the earth, by evil spirits dwelling in the skies.

I forget how the author explained the bad marksmanship of these spirits—who have so seldom hit even a baby—nor why it is that so many of these missiles fall in waste places of the earth. (Of course, the firing is done at very long range, and the spirits may still be hopeful of knocking over somebody, some day.)

The author developed his theory in a style which was, at least, sane; and, if I recollect, even showed some traces of humour—a quality extremely rare in those who produce eccentric literature. His book —which he has followed with another, also astonishing—may have been a hoax. In that case, the object of so much labour is still obscure.

A few months after publication, the author came into a public library, and—as authors sometimes do—asked to see his book. A copy was brought, and he promptly asked the meaning of the shelf mark: some letters or figures on the back. These symbols on library books, for convenience in placing them on the shelves, have a mysterious power to infuriate some people. The librarian, not aware that he was speaking to the author of the book, said that these marks indicated the class of "Eccentric Literature" —perhaps he may have said "Books by Cranks."

There was an instant explosion; followed by weeks of complaint, scolding, and entreaty by the author, who demanded that his book should be classed with those on—well, I cannot imagine what. Astronomical theology? Or did he believe that it should have a class all by itself, and that the older astronomies should be destroyed?

In the end, I think he got part of his desire, but not all. The stubborn librarians would not endorse his amusing treatise as orthodox science. They have that peculiar conservatism: they admit books meant to prove that Bacon wrote the Shakespearean plays, but refuse to throw out the ones which uphold the older belief; they take in works which show that the earth is flat, but they still let the brutal majority of writers uphold their theory of its rotundity.

Nevertheless, embarrassing moments will occur. There is, perhaps, somewhere a brave man who would say, when shown the eldest child and pride of the family:

"Madam, truth compels me to state that your son looks to me like a natural born simpleton."

And there may be in existence a courageous critic who can face an author with the remark:

"Sir, I have read your book all through, and I assure you that it is one hundred per cent. drivel."

For the most part, however, the cowards prefer to utter these things in print and at long distance.

Augustus De Morgan, the mathematician, and father of the novelist, was for many years a semi-official defender of science against the assaults of all the tribes of snipers who think they can square the circle, or upset the theory of gravitation, or solve the problem of "the number of the Beast" in the Revelation of St. John the Divine, or prove the earth not to be a globe. He called their notions "paradoxes," and finally published what is almost an encyclopædia of the theories of these schools of thought in a book entitled *A Budget of Paradoxes*. He also suggested for these theories the name of crotchets.

Gustave Brunet (calling himself "Philomneste Junior") was more frank in the title of *Les Fous Littéraires*, which is a dictionary of literary eccentrics. He includes, however, some illustrious names which are unjustly classed with the others—names like William Blake, John Bunyan, Poe, Swedenborg, and Walt Whitman.

The learned American criminologist, Dr. Arthur MacDonald, has made a study of "Eccentric Literature," in which he has examined several hundred books, and considered scores of authors. They are usually cranks, he says, but he thinks it more accurate and polite to call them "Mattoids." There are at least 284 writers who have produced eccentric literature, and among 227 books which he examined the greatest number dealt with theology. The subjects which followed, in order of number, were prophecy, philosophy, politics, poetry, and drama, and language or grammar. Twenty were on miscellaneous topics.

Dr. MacDonald points out their invariable redundance in language; their use of phrases in some peculiar sense; and their fondness for trying to prove that some great man was mistaken—Newton, for example; or that some great reputation, like Shakespeare's, is not deserved.

It should be added that, except in a scientific book, the work of most eccentrics does not admit of much discussion, for the reason that it is pitiable—the product of an unbalanced mind, or the pathetic attempts of a childish intellect.

Others, however, have been written by fairly normal persons, with only one crotchet. They are so pleased to get this into print, so vehement in expression, and so condescending towards all who do not agree, that we may look at their books without feeling that we are engaging in a cruel sport.

Few normal writers, indeed, are without some one eccentric notion. There is, for example, Alexander Woollcott, an eminent dramatic critic, a humorous and graceful commentator on the stage, and on literature, who has many excellent ideas and evidences of wisdom—such, for instance, as a taste for reading books about murder. Nevertheless, if, by some ill-chance, the subject of *croquet* is mentioned in his presence, the eyes of this poor gentleman light up with the fire of fanaticism, as he seriously argues that this game is a fit pastime for adult human beings. Others there be who praise *cats* as household pets.

The titles which the crotcheteers give their books are often as mystifying as the contents. Here is

"*The Road Made Plain to Fortune for the Million; or, The Popular Pioneer to Universal Prosperity.* By Alex. Lookup, the Extraordinary Poet-Author, Inspired Romance Writer, and Glorious Social Reformer; by an Effulgent Discovery, setting forth the elements for a Heavenly and Consummate Civilization. Edited by Thos. Ward, M. D."

This was published in New York in 1860, and its meaning is a problem. Perhaps the solution is found in a subtitle: "The Road to Universal Supernal California." Apparently in 1860, as now, all difficulties may be solved by moving to California.

Near this, on the shelf, was "*The Discovery of Discoveries,* Climaxingly Collated in the Month of Una-and-her-lion (1908) inclusive of August; and fulfilling 'The Message of Ishtar.'" The mystery which surrounds this book is insoluble, on the title page and everywhere else.

The *Letters to 'Squire Pedant, in the East* is not a crank's book at all. Its purpose is an odd one, but the author knew perfectly well what he was about. He called himself "Lorenzo Altisonant," which

was fully as pleasing as his real name: Samuel
Kleinfetter Hoshour. The second edition appeared
in Cincinnati in 1856; my enthusiasm is not sufficient to start me on a search for the first edition.

Mr. Hoshour's object was to teach the young
the meaning of long words, and especially those of
classical origin. Probably self-amusement, and a
little display of knowledge, were also among his
motives. He describes his travels in the Western
states in a series of letters, employing no short
word where he could help it. Here is his introduction:

Sylvanville, Occident, June 1, 1842.
SQUIRE PEDANT,—DEAR SIR; At my decession
from you; your final alloquy, and concinnous deport laid me under a reasonable obstriction to im-
part to you a pantography of the occidental do-
main upon which I had placed my ophthalmic
organs. I now merge my plumous implement of
chirography into the atramental fluid, to exonerate
myself of that obstriction.

He visits a Millerite* camp meeting at "Obstreper-
ousville," and begins with a description of the
preacher:

"The anteriority of the officiating homilist's

---

*An absorbing book about the Millerites is *Days of Delusion*, by Clara
Endicott Sears. 1924.

existence had been rather sinuous and protean. His juvenility had been maculated with many vicious extravagations. At the termination of his adolescence, he became a fustilarian, a scambler, a literator, and an omnivagant under the profession of a bletonist. By an esoteric and supernal influence he was speedily transformed into a pietist, and he transferred the acumen of his visual powers from subterrene objects, into the cryptic parts of the hagiography. . . . His hierology was on the appropinquation of the empyrosis of this macrocosm, based on the fatidical part of the hierography. . . . "

The visitor then looks at the audience:

"In juxtaposition to this, were dualistic departments for the gent, farandly and debonair auditors; and posterior to these were two for the bisexuous rabblement.

"The male department was fraught with fatours, fop doodles, boolies, louts, clawbacks, kickshoes, petit-matres, ragabashes, rakehells, rampallions, bumpkins, jackanapes, and wassailers. The feminine department was stocked with jilts, jillflirts, malkins, mauthers, modders, tomrigs, demireps, and gamerstangs. These occupants of the two departments mutually nictated at their lemen, and exhibited the most derisory deport toward the homilist."

The preacher spoke to his disreputable audience in severe terms:

DR. PETRIE'S PROPOSAL
DRAWN FOR PETRIE'S *RULES OF GOOD DEPORTMENT*

SHE CUTS THE TWIG, AND HER HUSBAND IS PRECIPITATED OVER THE FALLS OF NIAGARA.

ELEANOR BURTON'S HAPPY THOUGHT

THE FEARFULLE/S OF ELIZABETH MASTERS.

THE FEARFUL LEAP OF ELIZABETH MASTERS

"O! ye faitours, rakehells, rampallions, wassailers, jillflirts and demireps! what hortation shall I import to you? You all lie under the divine execration, and your subastral existence is truly temporaneous. Divest yourselves of your imbonity, incogitancy, and malversation; bonity is impetrable; perpend your longinquity from eupathy, and the inenarrable sequences of your impreparation for the apropinquating catastrophe. O! ye petit-matres, conculcate the fulgid ornature of your persons, and suppress your nugacities and stultiloquy, and ye kickshoes, cease your tripudiations; and ye wassailers elide your costrels and dengeate yourselves of your vinolency; and ye clinquant jillflirts, abject your elamping and bombycinous habiliments, and your bijous, and cease from your irrational calamistrations. . . ."

Six or seven years ago there was published at Wilkes-Barre a very long book with the title: *Hadhuch-Anti Hell-War; Monarchy's Victory Constitution's Triumph Tribute's Annihilation.*

It will probably leave most of its readers as mystified as Alice after she first read "Jabberwocky," when she was only able to conclude that somebody killed something.

It is apparent that the author, G. V. Damiano, had been pondering upon *The Divine Comedy* of his great compatriot, and had boldly essayed something like it, rather rashly choosing to write in a language in which he was not altogether at ease.

He outlines his first chapter in three sections:

"1. How God assembled his council and how Legù were commanded to enlist me as imperial militia.
"2. How God's respectable federal government announced me the promulgated Authority and how it shown its Universal garden.
"3. How Legù surprised and conquered me in Amo's State."

A later chapter is announced in this wise:

"1. How I opened the infernal vestibule and entered into the first Bulge.*
"2. How I been attacked by certain caravans of Cows.
"3. How I discovered the first infernal Spy."

The Cows, it appeared, were "without horns and with sweet breath. But they were making a terrible bawl in an order to thunder the entire Bulge."

The hero goes on from Rings to other Bulges, in one of which he encounters Dante and Virgil. Much is said about an important personage known as "King Vegy of this Reign." Then occurs an incident which raises the question whether the

---

*Probably the author's too free translation of Dante's *bolgia*.

author's inspiration at this point came not so much from Dante as from Mr. James Branch Cabell:

"I met a lady (1) with her hairs (2) dishevelled and naked (3) herself. But an (4) Authority were beating her and saying to her that she would not appear well and making a scandal."

The situation recalls the embarrassing conduct of Miss Wilberforce, in *South Wind*, who used to disrobe at the most inappropriate moments.

Another "Authority were going to fetch a mantle to cover her. In the mean time the two Authorities were begging her that she would look better to cover herself. Then they were trying their best efforts, but they were unable to succeed their scope."

Finally, the hero threatens her with his sword (Mr. Cabell, again?) and she obeys.

Soon—after two or three hundred more pages—the climax approaches, and we read "How Legù instructed me and directed me toward the infernal door." In the eleventh or twelfth Bulge he has a conversation with a Princess:

"Hey Princess thou shalt not be joyful of my beautifulness as the nature has performed. Also thou shall not enjoy thyself having me near thee. All the consequences between us are to yield my pass and for this beg thee; otherwise one of us has to get his fate. . . . ."

In Chapter III, he enters "Sensy's Garden,"

and a little later "Sensy's first fort." Sensy himself "fled into the intern of his camp" and "Prepared to refrain my advance."

Nevertheless, he seems to make progress, for we find him describing:

"How I met the first Angel and how I choiced her."

A little farther along on his pilgrimage he had a less happy experience; he "met an Angel of poor quality of feminine sex" and this one, apparently, he did not "choice." For, "seeing her insolvency" he "left her there and departed."

Next, we find him appearing before "Poty's Tribunal," for what reason is not clear. There begin to be many references to the "Government of the Universal Cradle."

In the second part of the book, the author tackles the subject of the Universe and describes its form.

"His form is uniformly oblong-globular as that of the actual Egg."

There is a chapter on Reptiles, distinguishing reptiles with "sweet poison" from the others which carry "sour poison," and there are whole sections devoted to "Crasis" "Apocope" and "Euphony."

The last is always a favourite topic with certain writers. It has the charm of obscurity. When the president of a corporation wrote from its headquar-

ters in an inland city, to the New York office, that
the employees should "take care to observe
euphony in business correspondence," it is said
that a violent argument broke out in the office, as
to the meaning of "euphony." One faction held it
to be the name of a Jewish holiday, while others
declared that it meant a panic on a ferryboat.

The author of *Hadhuch-Anti*, like many experienced writers, leaves off where he began, and in
his last sentence brings his readers into the same
perplexity with which most of them read his opening words. His final advice is to

"See Anti-Hell Sensy's State."


Edwin H. Tenney, the orator who delighted the
citizens of Rome, Tennessee, on Independence
Day, 1859, made one earlier appearance of which
the record survives. He addressed the Young Men's
Association at Great Bend in 1858. He spoke on
"The Romance of Reform."

Mr. Tenney loved language as such. The meaning of words did not concern him. The question
in his mind was, did they sound well?

He remarked, at one point in his speech:

"Such a theme needs no epitasis. It needs no
amphitheatre with its Ignatius irritating the lions
to accelerate his glory. It needs not the inflexibility
of a Laurentius—or the suavity of a Pionius for its
apodosis."

His concluding paragraphs were these:

"Young men are *crowbars* and *minions* at the fulcrum of life—not pigmies or hollyhocks. It is the sinewed intellect, the sympathetic beat and ingenuousness that vamps a nationality, and whets its sensibilities. *You* then head the van whose plasmatic front can sway an universe. You behold in our national flank and rear—Minos and Rhodomanthos—Neros and Domitians beckoning you to the crooked policies of mistaken wisdom—dictating conjectures and issues by desperation and life—sheltering speculations and blemishes behind beauty and hope—and flooding our land with isms of vipers—but to seduce affections and macerate your brains.

"Would you remove these Senacheribs from Amaranthus—then become Melachthons in reforms not Catalines of your country. Better banish—like Lycurgus—politician and poet rather than not tear from our wheels this drag-chain of Romance which is the pabulum of fancy and nursery of woe.

"Yes, be conservative—be democratic—weigh possibilities and conjectures on steel-yards of the Union—and when the reviving embers of freedom have luminated with halcyon reminiscences your rout to the grave—with 'Non mihi sed populo' on your banners—immortality will welcome you as guest in another city where like Mahomet you can exclaim my wounds are as resplendent as vermilion and odiferous as musk."

Collections have been made of Baboo English—of the strange writings of the Hindoo with a European education which was still imperfect. The whole subject has been attractively presented, with little exaggeration, in Mr. Anstey's *Baboo Hurry Bungsho Jabberjee, B.A.*

To find a serious effort of one of these learned East Indians, in English verse, is, however, rather novel. It is called:

"A Genial Anecdote, forming an Episode illustrating a mysterious fracas between Royal spouses and peace. By Dr. Ram Kinoo Dutt. Retired medical officer on pension."

It was published in 1884 at Chittagong.

Dr. Dutt explains at the beginning of his epic poem that

"The ancient mugal Emperor Jajandar Shah
  Had weded the daughter of a Persian Pasha."

He then describes the charms and accomplishments of the bride:

"Her symphonicus poems were admired by all
  Her scientific idea had hardly a rival,
  Her beauty was standing the best of daylight,
  Had shining hue as well as moonlit night.

Her mirthful healthy mouth, teeth, and lips
Were literally dancing when sweet love creeps,
Her languished weast plumper thigh tender tiny
    feet
Were more atrocious against those once them
    met.
Her slender fingers were under middle height
Hardly pressed sweet heart with their weight."

The marriage of this prince and princess was
very naturally celebrated with what Mr. Tenney
would call "Nuptial orgies." During this festival,
someone chanted a

### SONG UNDER NATIVE TUNES AND DANCES

The dadalian deep dalliance
Sooner subdued sombre silence
Succeeded concupiscence well a day
There a ballet helter skelter,
Had a vice-versa encounter
There a laughter proved philter in vis-a-vis play.

There was also an

### ODE

Morning is dawning in the east
Sun is shining in his golden nest,
Artificial vermilion on the cheeks
Of ladies who are my rare guest,

Surpassed the solar golden hue.
Came on contact along at least
Iced cream crimsoned with rashberries
Made sapid beverage under hest,
Having overspread with the blushes
Look them served in the feast
Happiest sovereign moving on.
Jumped and kissed his dearest.

That these lines were sung "under native tunes" seems fortunate, for I should pity the composer who tried to set them to any music as we understand it. The statement that iced cream crimsoned with rashberries made a sapid beverage—either under "hest" or otherwise—seems a doubtful statement. Perhaps, however, Dr. Dutt, like Mr. Tenney, relied more on euphony than anything else. The verses which follow seem to indicate that this is true.

### DISTICH

Sing blethely, dance blethely,
  slowly, slowly, slowly, slowly.
With lower extremities undulating
  passed lowly, lowly, lowly,
Under sound of music and crankle
  of fine golden bangles, bangles,
Advancing forward turning backward
  when each waggles waggles.

This choral celebration of the wedding had a profound effect upon the Imperial bridegroom. As Dr. Ram Kinoo Dutt expresses it, in one couplet:

"Imprinting repeated kisses over
    angelic featured face,
His Majesty collopsed with
    eloquence and grace."

# SIDE-WHISKERS AND SEDUCTION

# CHAPTER IX

### SIDE-WHISKERS AND SEDUCTION

THE wronged and suffering maiden is a perpetual figure of distress. From the time of the old ballads down to the plays of Henry Arthur Jones she kept the light of her fallen day about her, as successfully as, in Walter Pater's belief, did Mona Lisa. Nowadays, she has gone out, and in novels and plays it is the innocent young man who has to be defended against the ravening flapper.

She will come back. There are signs that the great Victorian Age begins anew. The household decorators are yearning for it, and have already foisted upon us wax flowers, glass dingle-dangles, and other symbols of the antimacassar period. Mr. Eugene O'Neill, the most progressive of dramatists, has returned to the use of the *aside*, the silliest of the old theatrical conventions. I predict that within ten years, we shall once more see, in stories and in plays, girls who swoon frequently, girls of unbelievable and cast-iron virtue, pursued by rascally seducers with moustaches and side-whiskers. And it will be discussed as an interesting experiment in modernism.

From about 1850 to 1874—no, longer than that: at least until 1886, these girls had a dreadful time. Never had they so many seeming protections as in that era, never were they so begirt with the armour of righteousness. In their homes they were fortified by religion; parents and elders were addicted to giving moral advice on every possible occasion. The maidens themselves were the wariest and most suspicious: they smelt evil everywhere.

Their own persons were protected as never in history: crinoline and horsehair, wire and steel, pantalette and corset and bustle, basque and bodice, boot and glove, together with ribbons and bonnets which were so forbidding as to seem to discourage all gallantry. Yet the shore was covered with wrecks.

We who believe in the good, old times, must never examine the printed records. If we do, we may be stricken with doubts that the present is the Age of Sin.

My authority for this sad discovery in the sociology of the past is my collection of pamphlets, and especially those issued by the Messrs. Barclay & Co., of Philadelphia. This firm knew of some events which were sufficient to draw tears from any group of gallery gods.

For example:

LIZZIE NUTT'S SAD EXPERIENCES.
A Heart Broken, and a Family Plunged in Grief.
WRECK AND RUIN!
THE SHOOTING AND TRAGIC DEATH OF
NOBLE-HEARTED CAPTAIN NUTT.
LIZZIE'S BRAVE FATHER,
Who Flinched not, like a True Soldier, to die in Defence of
his Daughter's Honor
THE GREAT DUKES TRIAL
At Uniontown, Pa.

There is also *Another Broken Heart!* as it is called upon the cover, where there is a picture of the "alleged Pistol Scene between Rev. J. S. Glendenning and Miss Mary Pomeroy." The full title is:

POOR MARY POMEROY!
THE JERSEY CITY MUSIC TEACHER.
ALSO,
A FULL AND AUTHENTIC ACCOUNT
OF THE
Trial of Rev. John S. Glendenning
BEFORE THE
AUTHORITIES OF PROSPECT AVENUE CHURCH.
STARTLING DETAILS AND CURIOUS STATEMENTS.
WHAT A LADY SAW ONE NIGHT.

It should be said that Dr. Glendenning was cleared of the charges, by a pretty narrow vote of his presbytery, but they found him guilty of "unministerial and unchristian conduct" and severed his connection with the Church. By vote of 19 to 2 they decided that he did not actually point a revolver at poor Mary Pomeroy to make her sign a paper.

Unrelieved gloom marks the story of *"Elizabeth Masters, the Doubly Affianced;* Being the Life of a Southern Belle: or the Terrible Consequences of Being Betrothed to Two Lovers at Once."

Depressing also is *"The Sad Case of Mrs. Kate Southern!* The Beautiful Virtuous Georgia Wife, who being Maddened to Insanity by the Outrageous Taunts of a Bad Woman who had Enticed Her Husband Away, Killed Her. After Terrible and yet Romantic Adventures during her Flight, she was Arrested, Tried, Convicted, and Sentenced to be Hung."

The appalling wickedness of city life, and the especial depravity of New York, is always such a gratifying topic in the rural districts that the news dealer, or keeper of a general store in the country, found it easy, even in 1852, to sell his copies of:

THE
STARTLING CONFESSIONS
OF
ELEANOR BURTON;
A THRILLING TRAGEDY FROM REAL LIFE.
EXHIBITING
A DARK PAGE
IN THE MANNERS, CUSTOMS, AND CRIMES OF
THE "UPPER TEN" OF NEW YORK CITY,
BEING
A FULL AND AUTHENTIC DISCLOSURE OF THE
MYSTERIOUS
AFFAIR IN REGARD TO WHICH SO MANY PARA-
GRAPHS
HAVE APPEARED IN THE PAPERS OF LATE

Eleanor was a thoroughly good girl, of "polished manners, elegant exterior, and connected with one of the first families of New York." Her father was a wealthy merchant with a princely mansion, in fact, two princely mansions: one in the country. She was betrothed to Eugene Burton, her father's chief clerk, whose "form was graceful and yet manly, his complexion a rich bronze, his eyes dark, penetrating, and melancholy."

If these young ladies had been allowed to follow their tastes in the direction of noble young clerks, honest tradesmen, or superb sons of magnificent farmers, there would not have been so many tragedies and confessions. Always, instead, they were forced to take up with some snake of a millionaire.

In this instance he was called Mr. Morton, and he was very disagreeable.

"Over fifty years, corpulent in form, bald-headed, his florid face bore the undeniable traces of a life exhausted in sensual indulgence."

Mr. Morton held the wealthy merchant's note for three hundred thousand dollars, and the payment of this would leave the wealthy merchant bankrupt. Moreover, as Mr. Morton had discovered, Eleanor's father had been dabbling a little— yes, more than a little—in the African slave trade. One word to the Government, and her venerable parent would—to use his own language—have to "rot in a felon's cell."

The alternative which Mr. Morton proposed
will be clear. The Government did not hear about
the slave trading. Says Eleanor:

"The next day we were married. In the dusk of
the evening four figures stood in the spacious parlour of my father's mansion, by the light of a
single waxen candle. There was the clergyman,
gazing in dumb surprise upon the parties to this
ill-assorted marriage; there was my father, his
countenance vacant almost to imbecility—for the
blow had stricken his intellect; there was the bridegroom, his countenance glowing with sensual triumph;—and there was the bride, pale as the bridal
dress which enveloped her form about to be
sacrificed on the altar of an unholy marriage. We
were married, and between the parlour and the
bridal-chamber one hope remained. Rather than
submit to the embraces of the unworthy sensualist,
I had determined to die even upon the threshold of
the bridal chamber. I had provided myself with a
poignard. But alas! a glass of wine, drugged by
my husband's hand, benumbed my reason, and
when morning light broke upon me again, I found
myself in his arms."

The married career of Mr. and Mrs. Morton was
according to the prescribed custom of life in New
York:

"He gave parties at our home, to the profligate
of both sexes, selected from a certain class of the

so-called 'fashionables' of New York. Revels prolonged from midnight until dawn, disturbed the quiet of our mansion; and in the wine-cup and amid the excitement of these fashionable but unholy orgies, I soon learned to forget the pure hopes of my maidenhood. Three months passed, and no word from Eugene. My father meanwhile was sinking deeper every day into hopeless imbecility. At length, the early part of summer, my husband gathered together a party of his fashionable friends, and we departed on a tour to Niagara Falls."

At Niagara, however, things were no better. They stayed at the —— Hotel, "and the orgies which had disgraced my father's mansion were again resumed." Mr. Morton was one who had to have regularity and system in his orgies.

The writer does not give us any details, but so far as can be discovered the orgies consisted of drinking champagne and singing songs. The result was appalling.

The orgies bored Eleanor, and she began to take moonlight walks, near the Falls. Putting on a bonnet and veil she would walk out to Goat Island, and thence to Luna Island. One evening she met her affianced lover, Eugene, who was also looking at the moon. He had arrived, in a mysterious fashion, *via* Mexico. She dared not tell him of her marriage, and they fondly embraced and exchanged tender words, before they parted.

Eleanor returned to the edge of the Falls, determined to commit suicide. But the chorus of a drinking song fell upon her ears: Mr. Morton had come out to the Falls, bringing his orgy with him. At least, "he was confused and excited by the fumes of the champagne." As he stood looking over, his wife had a bright idea. Here is her version of it:

"His attitude, the cataract so near, my own lost and hopeless condition, all rushed upon me. Veiling my face, I darted forward and uttered a shriek. Startled by the unexpected sound, he turned, lost his balance, and fell backwards into the torrent. But as he fell, he clutched a branch which overhung the water. Thus scarcely two yards from the brink, he struggled madly for his life, his face upturned to the moon. I advanced and uncovered my face. He knew me, for the shock had sobered him.

"'Eleanor, save me—save me!' he cried.

"I gazed upon him without a word, my arms folded on my breast, and saw him struggle, and heard the branch snap, and, heard his death howl as he was swept over the Falls."

The artist makes her cut the twig to help Mr. Morton over the Falls, so there is evidently a dispute about it.

She returned to New York and married Eugene. But, after a year, he began to wander to Philadelphia. Eleanor followed him, disguised as a boy, and

"THANK GOD, THERE ARE SOME SPARKS OF LIFE
REMAINING!"
(From: *Elizabeth Masters, the Doubly Affianced*.)

BEATRICE TRIES TO END IT ALL

found that he was preparing to elope with a girl named Ada Bulwer. Eleanor still had her "poignard," and her taste for disposing of husbands had been whetted by the incident at Niagara. She assassinated Eugene and again returned to New York.

Her subsequent career closely approached downright wickedness. She seduced a popular preacher, named the Reverend Herbert Lansing. She began to go in for orgies on her own account. They had rather a fascination for her, and she has left us a discriminating classification of the kinds of orgies:

"I sought the society of that class of fashionables to whom my husband—Morton—had introduced me. I kept open house for them. Revels, from midnight until dawn, in which men and women of the first class mingled, served for a time to banish reflection, and sap, tie by tie, every thread of hope which held me to a purer state of life. The kennel has its orgies, and the hovel, in which ignorance and squalor join in their uncouth debauch; but the orgies of the parlour, in which beauty, intellect, fashion, and refinement are mingled, far surpass, in unutterable vulgarity, the lowest orgies of the kennel."

This may be true, but there will be some persons to suggest that an orgy in which beauty, intellect, fashion, and refinement are mingled sounds like a rather pleasant party.

Eleanor, together with one of her friends, named Dudley Haskins, engaged in a hideous plot against the affianced wife of Mr. Lansing—a plot that brought them all into the depths of tragedy and seems to have ended in the suicide of Eleanor herself.

In order to brighten the gloom of the narrative, let us part from Eleanor Burton by reading her description of Mr. Haskins and his costume:

"Dudley was one of my fashionable friends, over forty in years, tall in stature, with a florid face, short curling brown hair, and sandy whiskers. He was a roué, and a gambler, and—save the mark— one of the first fashionables of New York. Dudley dressed in a showy style—blue coat, red velvet vest, plaid pants, brimstone colored gloves, and a profusion of rings and other jewellery."

The story of *The Great Wrongs of the Shop Girls* is so very painful that it will be best to say now, that it ends in happiness. Always, in these stories, there is a Seducer, with a moustache, and side-whiskers, but there is also a clerk, or a bookkeeper, who is the protector of virtue, and he also has a moustache and side-whiskers. The heroine, by some method or other, is instantly able to differentiate the side-whiskers of infamy from the side-whiskers which are enlisted in behalf of the celestials.

The story is called:

### THE GREAT WRONGS OF THE SHOP GIRLS
### THE LIFE AND PERSECUTIONS
#### OF
#### MISS BEATRICE CLAFLIN

How Miss Claflin became the White Slave in
the Gilded Dry Goods Palace of a Merchant Prince!
Her Incarceration in a Private Insane Asylum!
Two Years in a Mad House! . . .

Forced, by the financial ruin and death of her
father, to seek employment in a "Gilded Dry
Goods Palace," Miss Claflin* is paid five dollars a
week, of which fifty cents is deducted each week for
fines.

Young Tom Hilton is the son of the owner. He is
an evil man. His victims invariably jump from
Brooklyn ferryboats, their babies in their arms.

George Bentley is the cashier, and he longs to
protect the employees. They love and venerate
him, and give him a gold watch and chain on Christmas Eve. He respectfully admires Beatrice, and
pities her sad fate.

Beatrice applies to Tom Hilton for an increase
in wages. There are sickness and misfortune at
home. The illustration (see the frontispiece) shows
her modest and ladylike conduct, and it also clearly
indicates the character of the human viper who

---

*The author of this pamphlet trifles with real family names. His characters
and events are nevertheless fictitious.

seeks to take advantage of her distress. Beatrice is already a little depressed, since she has just visited the Morgue to look at the latest of Tom's victims. Here is the conversation:

"'I would not ask the favor, Mr. Hilton,' said Beatrice, 'were it not that I love my little sister so much, and I can't bear to think of her in a hospital ward.'

"'No, it would be a deuced shame,' observed Tom. 'Of course, we couldn't think of seeing her in a hospital.'

"'Thank you, sir,' said Beatrice, gratefully, 'I shall always remember your kindness. I can expect the advance, then?'

"'Well, yes. That is—you know—but you won't allow a fellow to talk. I've noticed for some time that you looked pale, and I felt sorry for you. Selling lace in a great store like ours is too much for you. You can't stand it. It will ruin your health. Now, it is in my power to grant your request, or extend you any other little favour. The Governor leaves all that sort of thing to me. I take a great interest in you. 'Pon my word, I do. There, don't get offended. I'm gcing to make you an offer. I'm getting ready to take a run to the West Indies on my yacht. There's a nice lot of young fellows, and some devilish clever girls going. If you make one of the party, I'll——'

"He stopped short, and a muttered oath escaped him. Beatrice had risen to her feet, and now faced him with flashing eyes. Coward that he was, Tom Hilton quailed and shrank back before the fiery eyes of the pure woman he had so grossly insulted. Beatrice stood regarding him a moment, and then with a gesture of scorn, she swept from the room; and not stopping to notice the sympathizing glance shot at her from behind the cashier's desk, rushed to the dressing-room."

She is instantly discharged, and matters at her house get worse and worse. Her injured sister—who has been run down by a horse car—needs things to eat, and it would be hard to get them if Tom Hilton did not continually send five-dollar bills, accompanied by imploring messages. At last Beatrice decides to succumb, and she pens the following passionate missive:

"Sir:—Will meet you to-morrow night in the ladies' waiting room, on the Brooklyn side Fulton Ferry, at half-past eight.

"B."

The next chapter is headed:
"Beatrice Determined to Make the Sacrifice,— Her Agony of Mind!—A Farewell to Virtue, if the Existence of her Poor Old Mother and Crippled Sister Depended upon It.

"She appeared to be in excellent spirits all evening. She sang for Ella, read to her mother, and it was not until both were sound in slumber that she dropped the mask, and with a horrible loathing, turned even from herself. She slipped off her house-dress, and putting on a light wrapper, relieved from their confinement her coal-black curls, allowing them to ripple like a cataract of carbon over her white shoulders. Instinctively she rose and faced her counterfeit in the mirror above her toilet-table.

"Through misty eyes, she saw reflected a face of wondrous beauty. At this time Beatrice had arrived at that point in life when woman, perfectly developed, has lost none of the freshness and colour of childhood. In the olden time she had been called a beauty, and men fell at her feet adoringly. Now, in spite of poverty and suffering, and the consciousness of coming shame, she was still beautiful. Beatrice was a brunette of the purest type. Her face was of that ravishing color and contour seen rarely in this cold clime. Proud, voluptuous lips, full with redness; a dainty nose; eyes that swam with hidden love, large dark brown, and fringed with lashes that swept the blooming and rose-tinted cheeks; a low, broad forehead, crowned by such an abundance of hair, jet black and curling, that now, when it was relieved, it fell far below her waist. She was above the medium height, not too slimly built, with well-set limbs and arms of ivory whiteness. Her hands were small and tapered, and her feet, though rather large, were finely shaped.

The unwonted fire brought out her Oriental beauty to its full perfection. At another time she would have looked upon herself proudly. Now her soul revolted at the contemplated degradation, and with a low, sobbing cry of pain, she sank on her knees before the mirror.

"'I am beautiful,' she moaned, 'and this beauty is to be my ruin—my everlasting and eternal ruin.'"

She cheered herself up as best she could, by thinking of the Morgue, and then proceeded to the New York side of the Brooklyn Ferry. Tom Hilton was already on the other side—he had been there since seven o'clock—smoking and cursing furiously.

On the way across, Beatrice changed her mind. She decided to welsh on them all, and jump overboard. This she did, and her act might have been fatal—nice girls did not swim at that time. But a stranger saw her, leaped overboard to her rescue, and soon held her in his arms.

"The tide was bearing him down the river, and with the inanimate burden in his arms, he was unable to breast the swift, flowing waves.

"'Quick! For God's sake, hurry!' he cried again.

"'Aye, aye! will be with you soon!' shouted the voice across the water, and soon a boat shot out of the gloom and rapidly approached them.

"'Here I am!' he cried, to guide the rescuing party, and the boat was soon alongside. He clutched the gunwale with one hand, holding his burden up with the other, and they lifted him wet and nearly exhausted over the ledge.

"'Saved! Saved from death! Saved from shame! Thank God!'"

The moonlight, shining full on him, revealed the bright and manly face of George Bentley, the cashier. He restored Beatrice and took her home, telling her, by the way, that he had discovered that she was the real owner of Hilton's Gilded Dry Goods Palace.

When he left her at her house, she allowed him to kiss her hand—or rather, when he ventured on this bit of boldness, she "did not repel this advance." She even went farther: she "conveyed by a gentle pressure the gratitude her heart was too full to utter." This drove the cashier into "an ecstasy of pleasure."

Tom Hilton, all this time, was still smoking and cursing, over in Brooklyn. But he was not through with them. He had Bentley arrested and sent to Blackwell's Island: they had caught him meddling with the firm's papers. And Beatrice, by the evil power of gold, was consigned to a private madhouse in Hastings. Only the mother and sister of Beatrice really profited by the Hiltons, for they were installed in "sumptuous apartments" at the Hotel Buckingham.

It all came out merrily in the end. George, on

YOUNG LADY'S OWN BOOK

LOVE AND SYMPATHY.

FRONTISPIECE, *YOUNG LADY'S OWN BOOK*, 1864

"ANNETTE"
FROM *THE GIFT*, 1845

Blackwell's Island, and Beatrice, in the asylum at Hastings had a disagreeable time of it for a year or two. Then the plots of the villains began to collapse, and in the last chapter, or the fifth act, everyone received his just deserts. Beatrice became the owner of the Gilded Dry Goods Palace and married George. Tom Hilton, after disasters in Wall Street, turned thug, and a ball from a policeman's pistol "went crashing through his craven heart."

But the mother and sister of Beatrice, who, for some mysterious reason, seemed only to prosper when vice was uppermost, again got the short end of it, and had to come home from the Buckingham.

# THE BAEDEKER OF BANNER ELK

# CHAPTER X

## THE BAEDEKER OF BANNER ELK

*T*HE *Balsam Groves of Grandfather Mountain* is a brief sketch compared with which Thomas Amory's *The Life and Opinions of John Buncle, Esq.*, is a painting upon a large canvas. Shepherd M. Dugger is the author of *The Balsam Groves*, and he has combined a romance with a guide book to the mountains of North Carolina.

It is, I think, the author's only published work, although it could not have met with a discouraging reception, since a second edition was required within three years. It is improbable that Mr. Dugger has been noticed, as he deserved, by any biographical dictionary. Although his style seems to be influenced, in some slight degree, by Mrs. Augusta J. Evans, the author of *St. Elmo*, he would be most unjustly accused of imitation, or any gross form of literary brigandage.

*The Balsam Groves* has had a small circle of devotees; now and then the number of them is enlarged and some dealer in second-hand books is importuned for a copy.

The whole title is *The Balsam Groves of the Grandfather Mountain: a Tale of the Western North Carolina Mountains. Together with Information Relating to the Height of Important Mountains, etc.* It was published by the author in 1892.

The second edition, as I suppose it to be, is dated 1895, and appears to differ from the first only in the frontispieces. Both are portraits of the author. In the second edition Mr. Dugger is shown after a lapse of years had somewhat thinned his hair and heightened his brow. The book has one characteristic which might possibly bring it within the notice of the collector: it is probably the only volume issued from this place of publication. Although printed at Philadelphia, it carries in its imprint the striking name of the little-known community of Banner Elk.

A gazetteer calls it Banner's Elk and tells me that it is "a post-hamlet of Watauga County, North Carolina, forty miles north of Morganton, and about five miles from Grandfather Mountain, 5807 feet high. It has a grist-mill."

Indeed, it has a grist-mill, and moreover it has one of the most delightful authors and one of the most charming, though unconscious, humorists in America.

Mr. Dugger succeeds in imparting some of the flavour of his work in the dedication. It is this:

To the Lovers of

THE SUBLIME AND THE BEAUTIFUL

And Especially Those Who Have Grasped My
Mountain Palm
This Book is Dedicated.

THE AUTHOR

In the preface he shows an accurate knowledge
of the average reader by assuring him that the story
is founded on facts. That is not only a safe but a
sagacious statement, since it is the exceptional
person who is without a lurking belief that for an
author to employ any imagination or invention of
his own is not only undesirable but almost indecent.

The story opens with two or three pages of description of the natural scenery of Watauga
County, after which we are ready for the entrance
of three of the characters. These are William West
Skiles, an Episcopalian clergyman; Mr. Leathershine, a gentleman who had been expelled "from an
institution of learning in the eastern part of the
State"; and a beautiful young lady, named Miss
Lidie Meaks. As she is the heroine, it will be proper
to quote the author's description of her.

"She was a medium-sized, elegant figure, wearing a neatly fitted travelling dress of black alpaca.
Her raven black hair, copious both in length and
volume and figured like a deep river rippled by the

wind, was parted in the centre and combed smoothly down, ornamenting her pink temples with a flowing tracery that passed round to its modillion windings on a graceful crown. Her mouth was set with pearls adorned with elastic rubies and tuned with minstrel lays, while her nose gracefully concealed its umbrage, and her eyes imparted a radiant glow to the azure of the sky. Jewels of plain gold were about her ears and her tapering strawberry hands, and a golden chain, attached to a time-keeper of the same material, sparkled on an elegantly rounded bosom that was destined to be pushed forward by sighs, as the reader will in due time observe. Modest, benevolent, and mild in manners, she was probably the fairest of North Carolina's daughters."

Exactly why Miss Meaks, the Rev. Mr. Skiles, and Mr. Leathershine were travelling through the mountains on horseback and seeking shelter for the night at the cabin of Tom Toddy is not altogether clear.

I should have explained that all this was upon "one lovely evening in the month of July, 1860, when Sol was shooting his last golden arrows across the mountaintops from his rosy couch beyond the horizon. . . ."

Their adventures during the night and the following morning in the rough cabin of Tom Toddy and his wife occupy about a chapter, and do not per-

ceptibly advance the narrative. We are introduced to a hunter, who has the extraordinary name
of Rollingbumb, and the author has a chance to
describe, not without some appreciation of the
humour of the situation, the difficulties of bestow-
ing the travellers in the same cabin with the Toddy
family. That this is all done with the utmost delicacy and the most scrupulous regard for the pro-
prieties may be indicated by saying that the author
cannot mention the fact that one of the Toddy
children has burned a hole in his undershirt without using a circumlocution like "the under-garment
that clothed the upper half of his person."

There is nothing in the chapter which has the
slightest resemblance to any of the wayside adventures which might befall a party of travellers
in a tale by Boccaccio or Smollett.

In the morning they all ride up the mountain,
but Mr. Dugger is quite unable to refrain from embarking upon his duties as the Baedeker of Watauga County.

His attention constantly wanders from Miss
Lidie to inform us that:

"From the base of this cliff gushes and sparkles
the coldest perennial spring isolated from perpetual snow in the United States. Its highest
temperature is forty-two degrees, and half a pint
from its unpolluted channel quenches the greatest
thirst created by an exhaustive climb."

This excellent spring serves a purpose in the idyl, for while they are resting beside it two other travellers join them. Miss Meaks recognizes them, and—the musicians in a moving-picture theatre would now play "Hearts and Flowers,"—"the beautiful rhododendron bloom that embossed her bosom now rose and fell with a deep sigh that pushed forward the elegantly rounded prospect behind it."

Any experienced Freudian would be certain that the author of *The Balsam Groves* had a decided bosom-complex.

The hero and his guide ride up. The hero is called—for Mr. Dugger's characters bear no mean names—Mr. Charlie Clippersteel. There are a few moments of light chat, and then the supernumeraries ride away, while Mr. Dugger himself is off upon a two-page description of the view. Everyone's back being turned, we are ready for the proposal, the moment for which every romantic writer sharpens his pen.

"'Miss Lidie, I offer you my hand, as in the days of yore, to help you up the rocks and steps of a path which, my guide informs me, leads through flowery beds and mossy dales like these.'

"'I accept your offer with thanks, Mr. Charlie; but you are not ready to go—you have not drunk the health you promised,' she said handing him the concave bark with a smile.

"'Pardon me, my friend,' said he: 'it cost me

four years in a foreign land to travel to the frigid zone of my heart, where the snows that ended the summer of love were lighted only by the flitting meteors of the borealis race. But your unexpected presence here to-day, which I could not avoid, has placed that icy region again under the burning sun of the tropics. Already the snows have gone, and their place is occupied by the water lily, perfumed with the spices and cloves and spreading its sweet petals upon my bosom. How can you drive such love as mine from its mortal habitation and leave my bosom empty with all but wondering pain? My heart is thirsty and you are its living fountain. Let me drink and water a desert that will soon flourish with the green bay-tree and the balm of Gilead.'

"'O God,' she cried, 'pardon the weakness of woman,' and burying her face in his bosom, her lachrymal lakes overflowed his garments with drops that were to him the myrrh of the soul.

"'It is pursuit,' she said, 'and not possession, that man enjoys, and now therefore the tender regard you have for me is ready to be cremated upon the pyre of my broken spirit, and nothing but an urn of ashes left to its memory.'

"'Never,' replied Charlie, 'never until God himself is buried, and the dark marble of oblivion erected for his tombstone, shall my person or my angel forsake fair Lidie Meaks.'"

After that, and for a while, the course of their love runs fairly smooth, and they roam about, picking flowers, sympathetically and learnedly described by Mr. Dugger as "ferns, and wild pinks, and the little evergreen shrub, Leiophyllum buxifolium."

Leathershine, of course, turns nasty. The lovers think that the presence of the Rev. Mr. Skiles affords an opportunity too good to be neglected, and they make the usual preparations. One of the mountaineers is sent to a neighbouring town for a marriage license. The party wanders here and there for a day or two, staying by night at the various hotels and inns of the county (see the latter part of the books for rates, etc.), and by day "satiating their æsthetic vision" with the mountain views.

It is not for me, who once lived for a year in the historic county of Buncombe, in these very hills, to deny that the scenery is worthy of all the praise which it can provoke—even the purple patches of Mr. Dugger are not to be discarded as exaggeration.

Mr. Clippersteel endears himself still more to Miss Lidie by addressing her at great length, with long, passionate speeches about blue skies and stormy sunsets, about "the rays of old Sol" and the blooming fields. He does her simple justice by admitting that she, also, has the gift of eloquence.

"Your sweet words," he says, "dropping like vocal roses from the gardens of language, heighten, if possible, the joy of the thought that you are soon to be mine. Your silvery accents, to which the trickling streamlet beside us plays a sweet accompaniment, tell me to rob life no longer of the bliss for which I sigh."

It is apparent that in the household of Mr. and Mrs. Clippersteel conversation will be upon a high plane. When the lady murmurs her doubts about having the wedding in the mountains, on account of her lack of a "wedding garment," her lover explains that—

"The foaming falls will lend you from their white spray a queenly robe, the benign woods will deck it with flowers more gorgeous than the artist can paint, and the harmonious melody produced by the combined musical agents of flood and forest will greet you."

This seemed satisfactory, and the wedding goes forward. A party of mountaineers come to attend the ceremony, and Mr. Dugger provides descriptions of two or three of them.

One is Miss Ada Clark, "a blooming girl of sweet sixteen, whose form was cast in neat proportion's mould. Her queenly hands, tapering and fair as the lily, were gloved with a pair of red mits of her own knitting, which exposed the ends of the fingers and the first joints of the thumbs.

"Her golden hair was like a shower of primrose petals falling, and her cheeks were finished with the artistic touches of Aurora's rosy hand. Her eyes were like the corolla leaves of the blue-veined violet, her nose was a posy to her face, and her pearly teeth sparkled with nectarean dew."

While the clergyman is reading the service the rascally Leathershine provides a sensation. He forbids the banns—causing an excitement which most of us have wished to share at least once. As a rule we have to be content with the accounts given by dramatists and romancers, like Mr. Dugger.

Here is his report of the incident:

"'If any man,' said the clergyman, 'can show just cause why they may not lawfully be joined together, let him now speak, or else hereafter forever hold his peace.'

"To the great surprise of all present, a sneering voice, on a different key from the thundering of the falls, was heard to say, 'I object.' This came from none other than Leathershine, who had resolved to avenge his defeat by vexing the occasion with this obnoxious objection, based as we shall see, upon an odious falsehood; and, the better to accomplish his design, he had concealed himself in the green of the steeps, so as to appear at a time when the groom could not contravene his purpose nor do him violence.

"'What is the ground of your objection?' inquired the minister.

"'She is engaged to me,' was the reply.

"No one can describe the trembling pallor that seized the person of Lidie. With eyes full of overflowing fondness, she looked upon him she loved, as if to say, 'I am innocent.'

"Her chin dropped upon the flowers that adorned her bosom; every nerve and muscle of her frame lost its energy, and she sank at the feet of the groom, not in the fashion of one who falls under the influence of excessive excitement, but like a pure woman borne down by the weight of a calumny perpetrated upon a warm life that no sin had ever tarnished.

"The copious pool, so near the fainting bride, was yet so far that not a drop of its pellucid contents could be had with which to bathe her brow.

"But the groom quickly produced from his pocket a little bottle of brandy, which he had carried, as a precaution, in case of accidents, and spreading a portion of its contents over her pallid face, the signs of restoration soon became apparent. The country folks had gathered round like the people of a city rushing to the scene of an accident, when those at disadvantage look over the shoulders of those in front to get a view of the within."

Then the bridegroom snatched up his rifle and menaced the intruding Leathershine. In a few minutes "the infamous dude" (as Mr. Dugger severely calls him) is in full flight, and the "nuptials" proceed.

"Mr. Clippersteel settled with his lovely wife in the city of Raleigh, where he had formerly resided, and the murmurs heard in that family were like the voice of a sun-lit tide embracing the tinted shells of the shore of love."

After which, Mr. Dugger writes the words:

"End of the Story."

This is only the end of Chapter V of the book. Chapters VI to IX form the guide to the mountain region. But Mr. Dugger is quite incapable of writing unadorned prose, and the reader of this section finds many a reward. One example must be sufficient. The village of Valle Crucis is described, ending with this paragraph:

"The very best rural board can be had at Valle Crucis, at reasonable country prices, with D. F. Baird, Sheriff of Watauga County, who lives in a commodious white house, where the air without blossoms with the odor of plenty's horn, and the within is adorned with a cheerful wife and three rose-lipped daughters of joy."

*The Balsam Groves* made its author famous and attracted some attention from the newspapers. Consequently, in 1907, another edition appeared, which showed the melancholy results of success.

As with the man who was told at the hospital that his wife was "improving" every day, until she died, so that he was forced to write in her epitaph that she died of "improvements," Mr. Dugger, in 1907, being an author of national celebrity, improved his book almost to the point of extinguishing its charm.

Gone is the heavily mustachioed portrait of the author, and in its place appears a disappointing picture of a spray of rhododendron.

The love story is still there, but the heroine is now dignified into "Miss Lydia." New characters are introduced, including an unnecessary person called Bodenhamer, who has long-winded conversations with Clippersteel about geology and about the square on the hypotenuse. There is also another gentleman named Clide Mumpower, who proves, at least, that the author's skill in discovering curious names has not abated. The tale is expanded, without being enhanced.

In the second section of the book, devoted to information for travellers, there is an occasional gleam of the early Duggerian manner. Thus, at Elk Park, we read that:

"Mr. E. P. Tatum has been in the hotel and livery business for a number of years, and has never failed to give satisfaction. Ben Jonson says: 'He that would have fine guests, let him have a fine wife.'"

And Mr. Dugger adds, with the significant aid of italics:

"Mr. Tatum has *fine guests*."

When, however, we reach Valle Crucis and look for Sheriff Baird and his fascinating establishment, we are coldly informed that:

"The very best rural board can be had at Valle Crucis with Mr. F. P. Mast, who lives in a handsome house on the thoroughfare to Blowing Rock, and only a two minutes' walk across the meadow from the Watauga, or at the buildings of the mission school, which are not otherwise occupied in summer."

Something, perhaps the embarrassing rush of patronage, following the first edition of *The Balsam Groves*, has caused the Sheriff to withdraw his name from the book, and devote himself to his legal duties.

# LILIES AND LANGUORS

# CHAPTER XI

## LILIES AND LANGUORS

Papa, potatoes, poultry, prunes and prism, all very good words
for the lips—especially prunes and prism.
—*Little Dorrit.*

TO GIVE a work of pure moral sentiment, united with the most elevated literary character, has been the aim. Grace in the style and refinement in the ideas, were inseparable from such a plan."

So wrote the editor of *The Opal; A Pure Gift for the Holy Days*, when that chaste volume appeared in 1848. And as she penned these sentences (I am sure she "penned" them, and doubtless with the quill of a turtledove) she composed a text for that flock of literary lambs, that mincing series of gift books which raged—mildly—in America for about thirty years, beginning in the days when our grandmothers were young.

What a flower garden of gentility they were, with names like so many sweet symphonies! *The Aloe* and *The Harebell, The Lily* and *The Violet, The Hyacinth* and *The Laurel*—their titles soon exhausted all the floral names which seemed sufficiently languishing and melodious. So there were

*The Ladies' Keepsake* and *The Ladies' Manual* (of "moral and intellectual culture"), and *The Ladies' Wreath*, and ever so many others besides— all for ladies.

The changes were rung on "Casket"—that atrocious word which was so strangely fascinating in the early decades of the Nineteenth Century. There were *The Casket,* and *The Casket of Gems,* and *The Casket of Love.* There were *Dew Drops of the Nineteenth Century* and *Drops from Flora's Cup, or the Poetry of Flowers.* There was *The Pearl, or Affection's Gift,* and probably one named for each of the precious stones.

*The Snow Flake, The Offering to Beauty, The Gift of Sentiment,* and *The Rose of Sharon* (most redoubtable of all for its longevity) fairly represent some of the other titles which appealed to one phase of public taste in the period when young ladies are supposed to have spent hours each day repeating the words "prunes and prism," to make their mouths small; and when nobody went to bed, but everybody retired.

The origin of the gift book and the literary annual has to be blamed upon Europe. They soon spread to England, where the first of them appeared in 1823. Within ten years there were sixty-three of them coming out annually, but by 1857 the fad had perished. In America the stream of these delicate volumes arose in 1826, swelled to a flood during the time of the war with Mexico, when about sixty were published each year, and ran dry before the Civil War broke out.

Mr. Frederick W. Faxon has written a bibliography of this odd bypath of literature with an introductory chapter distinguished for its correct appreciation. He says:

"By 1860 the American literary gift-book was practically a thing of the past, henceforth only to be found in attics, or second-hand stores."

How many attics and stores, how many old trunks and boxes, old walnut bookcases and whatnots, contain them to this day! Few are the families which could not unearth a copy of *The Christian Diadem* or *The Moss Rose* or *The Mourner's Chaplet*.

We may picture Christmas Eve at the "residence" of an American family in 1847. Dozens of whiskered young gentlemen converging upon the elegant mansion, each with a copy of *The Gift of Friendship* or of *The Young Ladies' Offering* or of *The Annualette* for the modest maiden whom he desired to please. And she, with perpetually downcast eyes—if we are to believe the pictures in the annuals—must have swooned under the weight of so many gold-edged leaves, so many pressed-leather bindings. The table in her boudoir (unless she called it a "bower") must have been stacked like a counter in a bookshop.

Could she exchange or otherwise get rid of her duplicates, as a bride to-day disposes of her six unnecessary cigarette cases, or the surplus dessert spoons? Suppose—if she ever tried to read these books—suppose she unmasked some of the infamies of the publishers, even in advance of the indefatigable Mr. Faxon! What did she do with a *Token of Friendship* which turned out to be identical in text with an *Atlantic Souvenir*, a *Moss Rose*, and a *Honeysuckle*, which were already reposing on the parlour table?

I think the answer is at hand. She did what a modern family does with luxurious editions, sets of Complete Works, and "Libraries of the Most Stupendous Classics of the Ages." She let their mere presence suggest—to the confiding—the literary atmosphere of the home.

Some dubious practices were customary with a few publishers of these seeming-gentle volumes. *The Magnolia* of 1852 might look like an innocent flower, but really it was the serpent under it, for it appeared with an *alias* no less than six times. With some popular gift books, the publishers and places of publication, the colour of the bindings, the name of the editor, or even the introductory poem or article might alter, but they went forth in thin disguise, again and again: now as *The Wreath of Wild Flowers*, now as an *Amaranth*, and now as a *Garland*.

This was by no means the rule. The commercial honour of most of the publishers is not questioned. They did procure fresh material and new pictures— I beg their pardon, *embellishments*. Some of the volumes represent the best which the period could furnish in printing and binding. And that is much better than the dress of many a book to-day. Nor is it fair to hold up their contents to undiluted ridicule. If you search through the hundreds of them which survive you will find it hard to discover anything outrageously bad. There is sentimentality, and a rather mawkish piety, but the savage theology of that day is absent.

Some of the annuals had a few contributions from famous writers; the books were then padded out with mediocre prose and verse. Others consisted of mediocrity unrelieved. Many a modern book, priding itself upon its lack of sentimentality, contains offences against grammar which would never have been permitted by the editors of the gift books. And if the annuals professed so much devotion to delicacy and refinement as to make us smile, it is fairly certain that the studied indelicacy of some modern writers will soon be exactly as absurd. It is, to-day, except to its practitioners.

The editor of *The Keepsake* may have written "a garden implement" when he meant a spade; a number of novelists to-day not only call the same thing "a damned shovel," but drag in so many references to it, under that violent phraseology, as to raise a suspicion of juvenility of intellect. The literary folk, who, like the two little girls in the anecdote, are going "down into the garden to say some swearwords" are becoming increasingly funny, and certain to be a source of mockery to their grandchildren.

*The Gift* of 1845 is a fair example of the annual at its best. The copy which I have seen is well bound in full leather, red and gold. Print and paper are good, and the contents include poetry or prose by Longfellow, N. P. Willis, Poe, and Emerson. It is probably not the first appearance of any of these contributions, but the fact of their presence dignifies the book.

The Poe item is *The Purloined Letter*, and reading it over again leads me to wonder at the critics who exalt Poe, as a writer of detective stories, at the expense of Doyle. I would prefer, of course, to think that the American was the greater of the two in this field. Certainly, he was the pioneer; but to compare *The Purloined Letter* with *A Scandal in Bohemia*, for instance, shows quickly which is master. Doyle's plot seems to owe one device directly to *The Purloined Letter*, but his story is, nevertheless, superior to Poe's. For Sherlock Holmes is a human being, a man of action and of interest, while Poe's Dupin is a bloodless thinking machine.

# THE
## ROSE OF SHARON.
### 1845

EDITED BY MISS S. C. EDGARTON.

BOSTON
A. TOMPKINS

THE SMILING SPRING
FRONTISPIECE, *THE DIADEM*

The illustrations in the copy of *The Gift* are admirable engravings, and the editor's taste is indicated by the fact that they are enumerated in a "List of Plates," not of "Embellishments." The portrait engraved by John Cheney, reproduced herewith, is notable as one of the few, in all these books, in which the subject is allowed an expression other than the usual die-away simper.

*The Young Lady's Own Book* of 1864 does not seem to be an annual, although one of this title had appeared as early as 1832. It is, in nearly every respect, at the opposite pole from *The Gift*. This reproduction of its frontispiece is of the kind which we associate with the gift book, but do not find very often. *The Young Lady's Own Book* was "an offering of love and sympathy," by Emily Thornwell, author of *Young Ladies' Guide to Perfect Gentility* and the *Rainbow Around the Tomb*. In her introduction she writes:

"I am not conscious of having been instigated by a single selfish thought or aspiration from the conception of my little volume to its completion. It has been with me, not a mercenary, but an eleemosynary effort; and, thus prompted, I did not think it unbecoming that, with grateful hand, I should take here a bud and there a flower, and binding them in clusters, place each in a humble vase of my own, and send them forth on the dovelet wings of their well-intentioned mission."

Whether the legitimate owners of here a bud and there a flower were in any way rewarded for the appropriation of their property is not shown. Miss Thornwell wanders through literature from Dante to Longfellow and selects with a liberal hand. She does make acknowledgment to about twenty living writers—not all, however, of those included in her humble vase—so it may be supposed that no crude act of piracy was committed by the author of the *Guide to Perfect Gentility*.

Her brief items, both prose and poetry, are grouped in sections, named "Esthetic," "Intellectual," "Affectional," and so on. The book begins with a "Proem," and each section has a prologue signed by "Rosalie Bell"—perhaps this is the author herself? It is a very, very flowery book, and there are selections entitled "A Shimmer from a Dreamland Wave," "What the Violets Did," "Maidenhood in Spring," "Female Dress," and "God Scatters Violets all Around."

The battles of the Wilderness, of Cold Harbour, and the march to the sea took place in the year that this sweet book was published. Thousands of "that fond and youthful sisterhood, the maidens of my native land," as Miss Thornwell calls them in her dedication, must have been terribly concerned for fathers and brothers and lovers. But no slightest trace of the rude subject of war gets into the book; doubtless the editor felt that it would be out of tune with her harmonies. Besides, there was no need to offend the enemy; some copies could, perhaps, be sold in the South.

The *Atlantic Souvenir* is said to be the first of the American annuals. It was first published in 1826, in Philadelphia, and it lasted for about six years—when it was swallowed by *The Token*. The copy before me is a neat little book, less than six inches in height, and bound in black leather. It could easily pass for a copy of the New Testament. Perhaps this is not chance. It has the engraved presentation page, or inscription plate, for the giver to write the name of the owner, together with his own signature. These plates continued in all the really swagger gift books and became worse and worse. There are five or six of the usual steel engravings, by way of "embellishments," and a score of anonymous contributions with such titles as "The Eve of St. John," "A Legend of the Forest," "The Spanish Girl of the Cordilleras," and "Biographical Sketch of Admiral Paul Jones."

*The Youth's Keepsake* for 1846 is a fair example of those annuals which were intended for children. Its stories seem rather more interesting to me— especially "The Ipswich Fright"—than do many of the honeyed love tales or disguised sermons in the volumes for adults. The pictures include some which are not without an old-fashioned charm, and others which are somehow offensive.

Charles Dickens—I wonder if he knew it—was a contributor to *The Diadem*, an undated copy of which contains the preposterous frontispiece called "The Smiling Spring." Dickens wrote "To be Read at Dusk."

Two brief stories in *The Diadem* attracted me; one called "Florence Dudley's Revenge" and one, "False Love and True Love," by Miss Power. In the first of these, a gentleman quotes Tennyson, only to evoke the chilling comment from Florence that—

"'Locksley Hall' is an exquisite poem, but written in rather an enthusiastic style."

"False Love and True Love" is a story of a young lady in France, whose mamma is credited with the finest derangement of epitaphs in the French tongue that I have encountered.

"'The Marquis de Montaland!' I cried. 'Why, he is much older than papa! *O Maman, chère Maman!* indeed I could not marry him!'"

"'Hortense!' exclaimed my mother, drawing up, 'You surprise me! M. de Montaland is not young, it is true, but what has that to do with the question? . . . You will have a noble name, a *salon* frequented by the most distinguished personages of the day, *des beaux equipages, des bijoux, des cachemires;* what more can any *femme comme il faut* desire?'"

Surely, any academy of refined young ladies who

FROM *THE YOUTH'S KEEPSAKE,* 1846

THE CRUEL CATASTROPHE OF MARY FINLEY
FROM *GOD'S REVENGE AGAINST MURDER*, BY MASON L. WEEMS

were lured into reading "False Love and True Love" could suffer no impairment of morale by studying Hortense's proper conduct during her two marriages. What was even better, they could pick up many correct French phrases from *chère Maman*, who was so obligingly liberal with them as to suggest that she had been egged on by some preceptress.

For thirty years, and even more, the *Amaranths* and the *Honeysuckles* and the *Ladies' Keepsakes* now trickled and now poured from the presses—a stream of thin syrup. Yet in that same period appeared *Walden* and *Leaves of Grass* and *The Scarlet Letter*. American literature was not suffering an attack of the vapours; it was never more vigorous. The gift books and annuals were the result of an affectation, a cult of elegance, and its parallel to-day is the cult of vulgarity which has flourished for a few years.

The week that this was written saw the publication of a book by an American woman who used no word if she could find for it a coarser synonym. Instead of being a display of strength, as she and a few devotees think, is this not also an affectation, a confession of weakness, a childish desire to shock Mrs. Grundy? This little renaissance of naturalism convicts itself of sentimentalism as clearly as do the authors of all those niceties and pruderies which filled the pages of *The Iris* and *The Forget-Me-Not*.

# "FROM SUDDEN DEATH"
## I

# CHAPTER XII

## "FROM SUDDEN DEATH"

### I

WHILE our great-grandmothers were having their tastes refined and their characters strengthened by means of gift books and annuals, our great-grandfathers, with their coarser masculine tendencies, were able to indulge the natural human liking for thrills and horrors. The floral gift book, whose heyday was the 1840's, arose, flourished, and declined in one generation. Its life, roughly speaking, was from 1830 to 1860. But the gallows sermon, and the pamphlet devoted to murders, to capital trials, to condemnations, dying confessions, and executions—these odd ephemeræ had a gradual and more obscure origin, and a longer process of disappearance.

They had been published in England as early as the Seventeenth Century.

The gallows sermon is associated with the Eighteenth and the early decades of the Nineteenth centuries. But the pamphlet devoted to the deeds of this or that notorious criminal may be found in tattered form, dated some time in the late 1600's, and it was still being printed almost down to our time.

In the small collection of them before me is:

*The Beautiful Victim of the Elm City Tragedy. Containing a Full and Complete Account of the Life and Death of Jennie E. Cramer,* which was copyrighted in 1881.

This was a tragic death and supposed murder in New Haven, which aroused a great sensation and is still remembered.

And *Red-Nosed Mike! Murder of Paymaster McClure and Hugh Flannaghan and Robbery of $12,000 on the Wilkes-Barre Mountain* which was published in Wilkes-Barre as recently as 1889.

But Red-Nosed Mike, whose portrait shows that the engraver has striven to do justice to his chief attraction—as far as black-and-white will permit— was one "of the Italian banditti." The foreign invaders were competing seriously with our native criminals; murder had lost something of its antique charm; and both this pamphlet and the one about Jennie Cramer have a dreadfully modern and vulgar look. Yellow journalism was arising, and these little books show its influence. I cannot bear to look at them in comparison with the fine, old, brown and stained title page of:

*The Life, Trial, Condemnation, and Dying Address of the Three Thayers* (1825) or that of:

*The Life of Samuel Tully, who was Executed at South Boston, Dec. 10, 1812, for Piracy.*

The murder fancier knows that the object of his devotion should mellow with age as surely as madeira. He is constantly beset to engage in a study of this or that contemporary murder, but only rarely does he accede. Let a crime show its merit, and survive the test of years, is his reply. He looks with languid interest at the columns of copy and the photographs reproduced in the yellow papers; he does not even care for the plan, with a cross to show where the body was found. But his eye sparkles at:

*"A Minute and Correct Account of the Trial of Lucian Hall, Bethuel Roberts and William H. Bell* . . . with [Hall's] Confession signed by Himself . . . and a representation of his Wounded and Bloody Right Hand. . . ." published at Middletown, Connecticut, in 1844. He pores over the:

*Map of the Country and Localities between Ebenezer Bacon's and the Residence of Hall,* with the marks to show all the points of interest in Middletown—Cat Hole Road, Elihu Plumb's House, Ebenezer Bacon's Barn, Old Roberts', Levi Yale's House, and "Mrs. Thrall's House where Lucian Hall lived." In these degenerate days probably not one inhabitant of that town could find any of these!

For information about a famous crime, modern

publications (such as the Notable British Trials) are superior to the old pamphlets, just as the sober, verbatim reports in a London newspaper give a far better idea of a trial than do all the boasted writers of headlines, all the feature stories, and all the productions of the sob sisters which the yellow press can command.

The collector of criminology—the genuine collector, who delights the dealers by purchasing with a lavish hand and never reading anything—this gentleman fills his shelves with old books and pamphlets and all the stock stuff on the order of the Newgate Calendar. This famous collection, with its variations and successors, is the dealer's darling. It has all the requisites which make him love a book: moderate rarity, high price, and contents which are frequently so dull and stereotyped as to be nearly unreadable.

The perpetual human curiosity about crime, sometimes condemned as low and degrading—if not actually indicating an intention to engage in foul deeds—is sufficient explanation of the existence and continued publication of the murder pamphlet for three hundred years.

The pamphlets developed from the broadside ballad. As late as 1865, at any rate, the broadside about a murder still appeared in England. I have seen one of that date, on which the doggerel verse purported to describe the confession of the famous murderess, Constance Kent, condemned to death, but sent, instead, to imprisonment, in that year.

Doubtless, the same matter was sometimes printed in pamphlet and in broadside form. It would not be surprising to learn that the *Three Thayers*, for example, also exists as a broadside—especially since it closes with a "Dying Address," in verses which add to the deep damnation of their taking off.

It is a fair suspicion that the gallows sermon was an ingenious device which enabled the publisher to get his pamphlet into homes where the bald history of the crime itself never would have been permitted. The reverend clergyman, of course, was quite willing, and with the best of motives, to have his moral discourse given the widest circulation, as a warning to youth to avoid courses which led straight to the gibbet.

When, however, we recall the specious excuses sometimes made, even to-day, for publishing and reading histories of crime, when we note the annotations in booksellers' catalogues, whereby "students of human nature" and other "scientific" investigators are recommended to these books, doesn't it seem probable that the father who would have shuddered to find his son reading *The Life of Samuel Tully, who was executed at South Boston for Piracy* might be edified to discover him with a copy of *A Discourse of Robbery, Piracy, and Murder;* in which Duelling and Suicide are particularly Considered; Delivered in Boston, February 21, 1819, the Lord's Day Following the Execution of the Pirates: by Thomas Baldwin, D.D."?

For although the youth might have to take a solid lump of theology, with precious little piracy to flavour it, still there must have been some sting in the discourse. At any rate, it was more to a boy's taste than anything else which Dr. Baldwin might publish, on transubstantiation or his other usual topics. As a sermon, it *could* be read on the Sabbath.

The reckless and unsanctified reader of a century ago could have, for a small sum, a wide variety of queer pamphlets, purporting to describe the horrors of crime, but all heavily charged with reminders that, after all, murder does not offer a suitable career for the young. He could gloat—if his inclinations were toward such action—over:

> ". . . lonely folk cut off unseen,
>   And hid in sudden graves;
> Of horrid stabs in groves forlorn,
>   And murders done in caves."

The egregious Mason L. Weems, inventor of the cherry tree and other Washingtonian myths, took a title from an earlier book, and wrote:

*"God's Revenge Against Murder; or The Drown'd Wife,* a Tragedy, Lately Performed, with un-

# NARRATIVE AND CONFESSIONS

OF

# LUCRETIA P. CANNON,

WHO WAS TRIED, CONVICTED, AND SENTENCED TO BE
HUNG AT GEORGETOWN, DELAWARE, WITH
TWO OF HER ACCOMPLICES.

CONTAINING

AN ACCOUNT OF SOME OF THE MOST HORRIBLE AND SHOCKING MURDERS
AND DARING ROBBERIES EVER COMMITTED BY ONE OF THE FEMALE SEX.

Page 16.

NEW YORK:
PRINTED FOR THE PUBLISHERS
1841.

LUCRETIA P. CANNON AND HER GANG FIRING AT THE SLAVE DEALERS

bounded applause, (of the Devil and His Court)
by Ned Findley, Esquire, one of the Grand Company of Tragedians in the Service of the Black
Prince, Who was so highly gratified with Ned's
performance, that he instantly provided him Rooms
in one of his own Palaces; Created him a Knight
of the most ignoble order of the Halter, clapped
bracelets on his wrists, and an ornament round
his neck; and in a few days promoted him to the
ridge pole of the gallows, at Edgefield Court-
House, South Carolina. . .

"O Reader dear, I give you here
    A book to look upon,
That you may pray, both night and day,
    Nor go, where Ned has gone."

This edition was printed by John Adams in
Philadelphia in 1808.

It will be seen that the Reverend Mr. Weems
was pleased to be waggish; indeed, "the celebrated
American historian, Doctor Ramsey," says of him:

"The Writer has the art of blending *instruction*
with amusement. While he keeps his readers in high
good humour by the frolicksomeness of his manner, he is inculcating upon them important moral
and religious truths, conducive to their present and
future happiness."

This account of the Findley murder ran through

many editions; and the picture reproduced here is
from the eleventh. The earliest edition I have seen
is the fourth, and this has merely a small but at-
tractive and probably imaginary portrait of the
victim. The artist invariably differs with the author
about the spelling of the name of Findley.

The Three Thayers—Nelson, Israel, Jr., and
Isaac—were celebrated in their day. They went
from Worcester County, Massachusetts, to a place
called Boston in Erie County, New York. Here, in
1824, they murdered their creditor, John Love.

> "Three brothers bent on crimes and blood
> In bold defiance of their God
> More monstrous than the savage fiend
> Have murdered Love, their nearest friend.
>
>     *    *    *    *    *    *
>
> "We long had plann'd the fatal deed,
> And on the horrid crime agreed;
> And none except the eye above
> To view our deeds, we murdered Love!
>
> "The wind that whistles by our ears
> Upon its wings his moaning bears;
> And tells aloud in accents clear
> That guilt will soon or late appear.
>
>     *    *    *    *    *    *
>
> "Once more I say to all, beware,
> Avoid sin's death-alluring snare;

Let every thought, and word, and deed,
Be governed by our Saviour's creed.

"Then shall heaven's bright glorious sun
Illume your path till time is done;
And when the last loud trump shall sound,
It's heavenly light your souls surround!"

With such verses were the wretched criminals turned off only a hundred years ago.

In the picture of Lucretia Cannon firing at the slave dealers, it is rather difficult to say which is Mrs. Cannon. It must not be thought that she was attacking the slave dealers because of any sympathy with the slaves. She preyed upon them as the modern hijacker preys upon the bootlegger.

Mrs. Cannon's father anticipated an industry of to-day by carrying on a smuggling business between Montreal and Plattsburg. She was married, at sixteen, to Alonzo Cannon, "a respectable wheelwright of Delaware." He died after three years, not so much in sorrow at her conduct, as from slow poison, for his wife resembled Lucretia Borgia more than the chaste Lucretia of ancient Rome.

Hers was indeed an abandoned character. She kept a tavern, into which were inveigled innocent slave dealers, only to be robbed and murdered. She died before the law could execute its sentence upon her, and the publishers sent this narrative abroad "that it may not only have the happy and desired effect of rescuing some misguided youth from similar offences, but save others of more ripened years from a fate similar to that of the wretched Lucretia P. Cannon."

John C. Colt, who appears in his prison cell, had a disagreement, as others have had, with a printer. The printer bore the illustrious name of Samuel Adams. Mr. Colt was so ill-advised as to put Mr. Adams into a box and endeavour to forward him to St. Louis. Those who are familiar with the famous crimes of New York will recall that a fire broke out in the jail on the day fixed for Colt's execution, but that he had already eluded the hangman by committing suicide. There is a fantastic legend that he escaped to Mexico.

The Eighteenth Century writings on crime, the broadsides and ballads, the pamphlets, the compilations like the Newgate Calendar, and the *Lives of the Most Remarkable Criminals* are quaint and curious in appearance and tedious in substance.

Hackneyed in style and heavily didactic, each essay seems to be run in the mould of the one before. The authors warn us over and over that we must not think that because they write about murder or highway robbery they are recommending them as proper occupations. The favourite phrase with which the brief items begin is:

*A View in State Street, while the Webster Trial was progressing.*

BOSTON IS WILDLY EXCITED

# Life and Letters

OF

# JOHN C. COLT.

PRICE 6 1-4 CENTS.

"The wretched subject of this unhappy memoir. . . ."

The usual closing sentence is:

"Having expressed the most heartfelt contrition, he resigned himself to his fate, and suffered at Tyburn on the 22nd of December, 1725, being then in the twenty-second year of his age."

The hack writers who composed these effusions must have been able to run them off in their sleep.

The collections of trials are much better. They are not always good stories, but they are the seed corn of good stories. Many authors, like Stevenson, have drawn upon them. One of the latest and most famous—because it was the work of a writer who afterwards developed a great prose style—was George Borrow's compilation: *Celebrated Trials*, published in 1825 in six volumes.*

Borrow's work was done under great pressure, and the fallibility of at least some parts of it is indicated in his treatment of the great case of Abraham Thornton. He took the contemporary, popular view of the prisoner's guilt. It has been shown conclusively that Thornton was quite innocent, and that the verdict of acquittal was just. There are later and much better accounts of this trial, and it is one instance of the fact that in the criminal field the advantage is nearly all with the modern writers.

*A brief version in two volumes, was published in 1928, skilfully edited by Edward Hale Bierstadt.

In 1827 appeared the first of De Quincey's essays "On Murder Considered as one of the Fine Arts." This was followed in twelve years by another on the same subject, with a postscript still fifteen years later. These masterpieces of grim irony constitute a declaration of independence for all who write or read about murder, and it is unfortunate that they are not better known.

De Quincey, writing a hundred years ago, is completely and delightfully modern in his method, and his work exploded a number of old superstitions. After he wrote it was never again necessary for any of his followers to assure their readers that murder is "an improper line of conduct." They could assume that they were writing for adults. He disposed of the stupid notion that any murder is interesting if it is gory enough. And he clearly stated the point (so often ignored by many of the writers of detective stories) that the interest in a murder is enormously diminished if it is established that the victim was an evil person who deserved his fate.

Finally, he told the stories of one or two murders in a manner which has been the despair of all who have followed him. De Quincey remains the master.

Forty or fifty years later Oscar Wilde used his pen in the composition of one essay about murder: "Pen, Pencil and Poison." But it is the English barrister, J. B. Atlay, with whom the modern method of writing about criminology may be said to begin. In a number of essays in the *Cornhill Magazine*, collected in 1899 in *Famous Trials of the Century*, Mr. Atlay told many readers of this generation the first they had ever heard of certain famous murderers: about Burke and Hare, Madeleine Smith, Constance Kent, and others.

Mr. Atlay's method was to write an honest history of the case; not to set up as a psychologist, nor anything else high-flown and beyond his reach. To adopt the phrase of Mr. Herbert Asbury, he did not try to analyze the criminal in the "I-think-he-thought" manner, but to chronicle events, and to have a scrupulous regard for the truth, so far as it could be ascertained from reliable sources.

Like his followers, he was between two fires of criticism: on one side from those of severely legalistic mind, who regard anything else than a full transcript of the court records as a descent into romanticism; and, on the other side, from the novelist, who would have the historian of crime take any liberties whatever with the facts, if in that way he can make a better tale.

There are a number of writers who think that this romantic and slightly immoral method of writing about crime is the correct one, and that not to inject from twenty to forty per cent. of fiction into the narrative is mere stupidity. In their view the subject is immoral, and the writer's dishonesty does not matter.

The six admirable books on criminology written by the actor, H. B. Irving, from 1901 to 1921, represent the conscientious efforts of an author who saw no reason why his subject should not be as carefully documented as if he were writing biography or formal history. His earlier book, *The Life of Judge Jeffreys*, was a "monument of industry," and in all his writing he disdained hasty and careless work.

In his *Book of Remarkable Criminals*, Irving first told the story of the midnight conversation of Tennyson and Professor Jowett, which has often been repeated. It may, perhaps, be given again, as it has a bearing upon a later and amusing comment upon Irving himself. This is the anecdote which the younger actor heard from his father, Sir Henry Irving:

"I remember my father telling me that sitting up late one night talking with Tennyson, the latter remarked that he had not kept such late hours since a recent visit of Jowett. On that occasion the poet and the philosopher had talked together well into the small hours of the morning. My father asked Tennyson what was the subject of conversation that had so engrossed them.

""'Murders,' replied Tennyson."

The biographer of H. B. and Laurence Irving, Mr. Austin Brereton, was grieved at Irving's interest in criminology—although he carefully read his works, as his chapter on them proves.

# THE
## LIFE,
# TRIAL, CONDEMNATION,

AND

## DYING ADDRESS,

OF THE

# Three Thayers,

## Who were Executed for the Murder of
### JOHN LOVE,
AT BUFFALO, N. Y. JUNE 17th, 1825.

———

BUFFALO:
PRINTED FOR THE PUBLISHER.
1825.

AN AWFUL WARNING TO THE INTEMPERATE.

# TRIAL,
## Conviction, Sentence,
### AND ONLY TRUE COPY OF THE
# CONFESSION
OF

# Catharine Cashiere,
MADE TO THE
### REV. JOHN STANFORD A. M.
Chaplain to the Public Institutions, of the City of
New-York the day previous to her
# EXECUTION,
Which took place at Blackwell's Island, on the 7th May, 1829.

Copy Right secured according to law.

Printed and Sold Wholesale and Retail C. Brown's 241 Water-st.

Here are Mr. Brereton's disapproving comments on the hobby of the two friends:

"One of H. B. Irving's best friends was the late Churton Collins, one of the leading Shakespearean scholars of the day, Chairman of English Literature in the University of Birmingham, a tremendous worker, a learned man, and a gentleman in the true sense of the word. He was held in esteem and affection by all who knew him. He was noted for the gentleness of his nature, for his lovableness. He was a perpetual burner of the midnight oil, rarely taking more than five or six hours' sleep, sometimes less. The study of criminology was one of his hobbies. In the pursuance of this study he made an exhaustive inquiry into the Merstham tunnel murder and into the Wyrley cattle-maiming outrages. He often sat up half the night discussing crime with H. B. Irving. Unhappily, he came to an untimely end, in 1908, at the age of sixty. 'H. B.' outwore his physical strength ere he was fifty. Would it have been otherwise if he had not so thoroughly and so constantly pursued such a morbid hobby as the study of murder? And could he not have put his fine intelligence and exceptional literary gifts to better use than perpetuating in print the deeds of criminals? In any case, although old gentlemen, be they poets or philosophers or otherwise, may sit up without doing themselves any harm once in a lifetime 'talking about murders,' the pastime would not seem to be a healthy exercise for a busy professor and an ambitious actor."

In America, the crime pamphlets and broadsides of the early 1800's were closely similar to those published in England. In 1830 the pamphlets reached their most charming form in those published in Salem and Boston on the occasion of the murder of Captain White, in Salem. There is a large, curious, and highly interesting collection of these pamphlets in the Essex Institute in Salem.

The writers of books of trials, like Jardine, about 1847, and Dunphy in 1867, seem to have thought that all the criminal cases worthy of notice were to be found in foreign countries. Jardine's book is almost wholly devoted to European and English crime; while Dunphy finds room for only two American cases out of fifteen.

Another idea which became fixed in the minds of American writers at an early period was that the only proper way to treat the subject was as fiction. This had many advantages: it allowed greater freedom of treatment, it brought greater financial profit, and it avoided any possibility of libel suits. With Poe, a writer of fiction, who desired, moreover, to suggest a solution of a murder, and point out the guilty person, it was natural to translate the murder of Mary Rogers to Paris, to rename her

Marie Rogêt, and to give all the other characters fictitious names.

In our time, Mr. Dreiser used a similar method in *An American Tragedy*—and this did not prevent him from drawing liberally upon the legal record of the actual case.

Other writers, however, tried various methods, some of them dark and strange. There was a school of pamphleteers (their work is described elsewhere in this book) who wrote novelettes about crime, and swore by all that was holy that their fictions were true. They went to some lengths to give an air of verity to their work. The probable explanation of this is that they were catering to readers who believed that imaginative literature is wicked.

Still others compounded true narratives, with a dash of fiction. Alfred Henry Lewis's *Nation-Famous New York Murders* is an interesting example. His crimes are real events; his *mise-en-scène* sometimes highly imaginative. Often, he makes unexplainable alterations in proper names, so that the border line between fact and fiction is blurred.

Celia Thaxter's *A Memorable Murder* is unsurpassed as an essay about an American crime. It appeared in the *Atlantic Monthly* in 1875. It is fact, with no admixture of fiction whatever, but so difficult has it been to understand this, that whenever it has been reprinted, it is always with collections of fictitious stories.

# "FROM SUDDEN DEATH"
## II

# CHAPTER XIII

## "FROM SUDDEN DEATH"

### II

THERE was a May morning, and a stile in a
meadow. It was very early—before three
o'clock—but as the country was England,
it was surely broad daylight. On the stile sat talking
a young man and a girl. They were still lingering on
their way home, and had been loitering through the
fields and lanes since midnight, at which prudent
hour they had left a country dance.

The girl was very pretty; a little less than twenty
years old. The man was four years older, rather
stout, heavy-featured, and a little awkward. In the
manner of his time—a mode briefly revived two or
three years ago—he wore closely cropped side-
whiskers near his ears.

His clothes, to use a novelist's phrase, were those
of "a young buck of the Regency," and to my intel-
ligent readers I do not need to describe what they
were. This is lucky, for I do not know myself. He
may have worn boots and "smallclothes," but, as
he had been to a dance, they might have been pan-

235

taloons and shoes. The date was only two years after Waterloo, so the pantaloons are doubtful.

It is possible to be precise about the girl's costume: a white "spencer," a white muslin dress, a dimity petticoat, white shoes and stockings, a straw bonnet with yellow ribbons.

There on the stile they sat and talked; apparently innocent, certainly obscure and humble folk; dwellers in a tiny village, who had just attended a dance at a little rustic tavern. Another guest, who had been seeing his sweetheart to her home, passed them, and said, "Good-morning."

The man replied; the girl hung her head and concealed her face under her bonnet.

Since we hear so much about the evil conduct of young people to-day; about flappers and their boy-friends; and about unchaperoned dances at road houses, it is instructive to consider this couple, sitting on a stile in the days when our great-grand-mothers were young, and when—so we are told—loose conduct was simply impossible. Young Abraham Thornton did not own a motor car, to facilitate mischief; nor did Mary Ashford carry a pocket flask of gin to promote flirtation. There had, however, been beer at the dance, and Thornton probably took his share. That night he had seen Mary for the first time, so there is something shockingly modern about the rapidity of their acquaintance.

The stately courtesy of more ceremonious days seems to have been mysteriously absent.

It is said—although he denied it—that on seeing her, and being struck with her beauty, he made a rude and highly improper remark about his intentions toward her, coupled with a boast about his conquest of her sister.

At all events, they danced together, and with another couple, at midnight, left *The Three Tuns* the place of the party, and walked along the London and Chester road, passing another tavern, pleasantly named *The Old Cuckoo*. A short distance beyond, the party dwindled, while Thornton and Miss Ashford were left during the remaining hours of darkness to their own devices.

These were not to say a *pater noster*, nor was the girl's conduct that of an "elegant female" within the definition of Mr. Collins in the then recently published novel, *Pride and Prejudice*.

It is one of the peculiarities of a celebrated murder trial that it suddenly lifts obscure folk into the most astonishing prominence, and one of its fascinations that it makes trifling incidents both important and interesting. A notorious murder will put an entire community under a magnifying glass, as, according to Hawthorne, the novels of Trollope did to the English countryside.

Mary Ashford and Abraham Thornton, sitting on

their stile, were the most commonplace pair, but
their adventures in the next hour were to amaze
the world, to alter the law of England, to confuse
judges and other great men, to furnish subjects for
learned treatises, moral discourses, and tragedies
for the stage. Sir John Hall, in compiling his account
of the case, found thirty-three items for his bibliography: sermons, plays, stories, and legal articles.

After more than a hundred years, after all this
discussion and writing, and after a Lord Chief
Justice and other great lawyers had taken a look at
it, even to-day it is not known what happened during the rest of that spring morning.

Of this we are sure. At four o'clock Mary Ashford
returned alone and in good spirits to the home of
her friend—the girl with whom she had left the
dance—and changed most of her evening clothes
for her workaday dress. Then she set out afoot for
her own village. Three or four hours later her bonnet, her bundle, and her white shoes were found on
the edge of a deep pool, in a field a mile distant. The
pool was dragged and the girl's dead body recovered
from the water. Near by there were footprints—
supposed to be Thornton's—there was blood, and
also signs, it was alleged, of a pursuit and a struggle.

Thornton was arrested. Public sentiment was
furious against him. He made no denial of some of
the facts, nor of the amorous episodes of the night,
but maintained his innocence of any crime.

On his trial he completely established his innocence, to the satisfaction of both judge and jury. They acquitted him in six minutes. By a number of reliable witnesses, who had met him on his way home, he proved that he was far from the scene of Mary Ashford's death. Sir John Hall says that of his innocence there cannot be "a shadow of a doubt."

Poor Mary Ashford may have met somebody else who attacked and murdered her, or she may have committed suicide. Both are most unlikely.

The probable explanation of her death is simple. She was tired and faint, and had had but little food for twenty-four hours. She stopped at the pool to rest and refresh herself. Her foot slipped on the steep edge of the bank and she was drowned.

Thornton's troubles were not ended with his acquittal. Public feeling was still strong against him, and a way was found to bring him again into court. The "appeal of murder" was not yet removed from the statutes; an heir of a murdered person, dissatisfied with a verdict of acquittal, could sue to make the accused again answer for his crime. This was done, and Thornton was once more put in prison.

His lawyers, however, found a complete, satisfactory, and delightfully humorous answer to this antiquated bit of persecution. The man arrested on "appeal of murder" had the right of the "wage of battel"—he could demand that the appellant fight him, "in lists sixty feet square," and if he killed the appellant, or could maintain the fight from sunrise to sunset, he was to be acquitted.

Now, Mary Ashford's heir was a cousin, a feeble young man, and not at all likely to prevail against burly Abraham Thornton. The latter, when the case was called, pleaded

"Not Guilty, and I am ready to defend the same with my body."

He thereupon threw a gauntlet upon the floor of the court, in token of his challenge.

The Ashford champion did not take it up; he did not even appear to admit his recreancy, and Thornton was forever acquitted. His neighbours were still against him, however, and he was forced to emigrate to America. It is said that he died in Baltimore in 1860.

I have heard that the "wage of battel" has been invoked in our own time, in Pennsylvania. A man proceeded against in a civil suit by a Y. M. C. A. secretary dared the plaintiff to the lists. The law was hastily consulted, and it was found that Pennsylvania had indeed neglected to repeal this ancient statute.

The defendant's attorneys instructed the Y. M. C. A. secretary that before entering upon the combat both contestants would be expected to take the prescribed oath that no spell had been laid upon their weapons, nor had *sorcery or witchcraft* been employed to protect the fighters. The Y. M. C. A. man adopted the course of Mary Ashford's cousin; he discreetly abandoned his suit. And Pennsylvania repealed the "wage of battel," exactly as England revoked that law, as well as the "appeal of murder," soon after the Thornton case was ended.

The *Trial of Abraham Thornton* is one of the volumes in the Notable British Trials series, now in process of American publication by the John Day Company. Eight or ten volumes of this amazing set of books have already appeared in this country. Others are scheduled for next year, and so on, until the forty-odd which at present comprise the set, have been published here.

New items are coming out, one or two a year; and the set ranges in time from the trial of Mary, Queen of Scots, to that of Major Armstrong, who was executed in 1922. With seven or eight exceptions, they are trials for murder. Each case has a substantial volume to itself. The method is to give a condensed report of the trial (even this condensation sometimes runs to 300 pages) introduced by a history of the case written by the editor of each volume.

The editors are distinguished amateurs of criminology, lawyers, or authors, including such persons as Andrew Lang, H. B. Irving, Filson Young, W. Teignmouth Shore, and Eric R. Watson. Two or three editors, including J. B. Atlay and H. B.

Irving, have died, and their places are being filled
by younger enthusiasts on this subject—as, for
instance, Miss Tennyson Jesse and Donald Cars-
well.

About eight of these trials have been edited by
William Roughead, whose work is widely known in
America. His *Burke and Hare* in the present group,
and *Jessie M'Lachlan* (not yet published in America), represent the high-water mark in a series in
which it is hard to choose favourites.

Even if one does not care to read all the pages of
testimony, in the report of the trial, the introductory essay, which is usually about the length of a
long magazine article, gives an interesting review
of the case. The illustrations, and the appendices,
with current newspaper comment, subsequent proceedings in Court, and the final fate of the accused
—whether sudden, at the hands of the executioner,
or in peaceful old age—make up a thoroughly well-
rounded story.

The volumes now available include, in addition to
the Thornton case, the internationally famous trial
of Mrs. Maybrick. When I was a boy, and when
tweaking the Lion's tail was in better repute than
it is to-day, it was good form every now and then
to pester the Government of Great Britain about
Mrs. Maybrick.

At that time, in the opinion of some of the
"Woman's Rights" party, any woman accused of

crime was probably innocent because she was a
woman. When, in addition, she was American born,
serving a life sentence for murdering her English
husband, the obligation to sign a petition to Queen
Victoria or to Lord Salisbury was evident.

Nothing could have been clearer, until the days
when that great light of knowledge was vouchsafed
to novelists, journalists, and poets, which enabled
them—in an instant—to know more about the
guilt or innocence of Sacco and Vanzetti than the
jury, the Governor, or the university president
who had *seen*, as well as heard, the witnesses.

Mrs. Maybrick's case is a puzzler; Mr. Irving
presents it with perfect neutrality, and two reasonable people may fairly, I think, hold opposite
views as to what was the truth. If she was innocent
she was the most unlucky soul who ever lived.
Those who have read her own book have read an
incomplete and (naturally) biassed account. Mr.
Irving very properly says that Mrs. Maybrick's
*My Fifteen Lost Years* deals "in its latter portion
with some of the facts of the case." The *some*
should be emphasized.

*The Trial of Oscar Slater* records a case which
was cited in connection with that of Sacco and
Vanzetti;—but merely by English papers, as a
reason why Britons should not be too loud in their
denunciation of alleged miscarriage of justice in
America. It has always seemed to me that Sir Conan

Doyle's defence of Slater was justified. Mr. Roughead does not take sides, but presents the history
with the impartiality of the legal historian.

At all events, Slater has been released, his case
heard on appeal, and the conviction set aside.

*The Trial of Madeleine Smith* is a new edition,
with a new introduction, by Miss Tennyson Jesse.
This celebrated trial of a pretty Scottish girl, for the
cruel poisoning of her lover, has always been a
favourite with murder fanciers. As the lover had
threatened to blackmail his youthful mistress, by
means of her love letters, there was little sympathy
for him, and the murderess escaped with a verdict of
"not proven."

The world has looked at Madeleine Smith aghast,
and yet with a certain admiration for her effrontery.
Miss Jesse, in her brilliant introduction, analyzes
her character and dwells chiefly on the love affair.
She does not trouble to investigate the girl's subsequent career, nor the vague rumour that she is still
living at the age of ninety, and in America! Madeleine's marriages; the identity of her husbands; the
causes of her marital infelicity; her social career in
London, and her acquaintance with William Morris,
Du Maurier, and Henry James seem to me subjects
which merited research. Incidentally it may be
said that her celebrated letters are now published
in full for the first time.

Little Major Armstrong, the "tea-time poisoner"

has a volume in the series. The Major dealt, with sly sociability, in arsenic—it was his specific for dandelions in the lawn, for an annoying wife, and for a rival lawyer.

A fantastic little devil—he so scared the rival lawyer and the lawyer's wife that they did not dare sleep at night unless one or the other kept watch, for fear the Major should come sneaking in, with his tiny squirt gun, loaded with arsenic for dandelions—and other enemies.

And there is that cruder pair of ruffians, Burke and Hare, who made the discovery that grave-robbing might raise blisters on the hands, and cause the operator to lose sleep—it was simpler and more satisfactory to convert living persons into subjects for the anatomical theatre by a programme of hospitable alcoholic entertainment, followed by smothering.

Mr. Roughead's treatment of this extraordinary case sets this volume in a class by itself. No one else, in all the serried ranks of Great Britain's crimin-ologists, possesses so many of the qualities which were displayed in editing *Burke and Hare*. For here are legal knowledge, an unwearied patience in mastering a large and complicated subject, excellent judgment in selection, and a vigorous and interest-ing style in the presentation.

The Notable British Trials, as they were pub-lished in England, in their red bindings, have been known to American lawyers, to custodians of libraries of law, and to some general readers and amateurs of the literature of murder. Their American publishers have done well to bring them over here; as they offer a dignified treatment of an interesting subject, in great contrast to a dozen or more trivial books of popular criminology which have been imported in the past two or three years. And instead of suffering in appearance by their transportation, they have actually been improved by it—witness their trim appearance in black and gold.

There are pleasant anticipations aroused by the announcement of forthcoming volumes in this series. It will be made convenient to read of the miscarriage of justice with Adolf Beck, and of the ancient case of Eugene Aram with its literary associations. There is that other literary murder case—of Thurtell and Hunt, as well as the story of Fauntleroy who, like Dr. Dodd, committed forgery and was hanged for it. The strange case of the Annesley succession is told by Andrew Lang. A modern trio, Neill Cream, Crippen, and G. J. Smith (him of the bathtubs)—have their volumes.

There will be the strange grim story of Jessie M'Lachlan, who rose to fame in Glasgow and died in Port Huron, Michigan; and the half-insane career of Ronald True, who once taught aviation on Long Island, but ended among the dance halls and night clubs of London. There is Mary Blandy, who was hanged with her hands "ty'd with black paduasoy ribbons," and Kate Webster roaming about to take tea with her friends, but carrying her bag with its horrible contents. There is England's "master burglar," Charley Peace.

There is that particularly contemptible traitor, Roger Casement, who tried to turn his humbler countrymen into traitors and was rewarded by being termed by them "a b——y rascal." The "b——y" represents a word considered very shocking in Great Britain; no one knows why. There are the strange couple, Bywaters and Mrs. Thompson. There is Samuel Dougal, who proposed a little excursion of "the girls" to attend his trial for murder: the girls being those who had constituted his harem. There is the wildly romantic tale of Katharine Nairn and her lover—a Thirteenth Century Italian intrigue set in Scotland.

And there is the story of Henry Wainwright, who invited the little ballet dancer, Alice Day, for a ride in a cab—an invitation whose acceptance was bitterly regretted, since there was already another and a ghastly passenger.

Writer of book reviews, sixty to eighty times a year, begin their articles with the grave inquiry: Why do people like to read about murder? After a discussion, in language that at least seems to be the result of profound thought, they come to the conclusion that people like to read such books because they like to do so.

Or the editors of Sunday supplements send their reporters to interview the psychologists on the subject. For it is well known, to the editors of Sunday supplements, that wisdom dwells, if anywhere, with psychologists.

In reviewing detective fiction, the owlish school are apt to inquire very solemnly why it is that learned and respectable men like to read mystery stories. That they do, they assure us upon their words of honour, and cite the great names of Gladstone, Roosevelt, and Woodrow Wilson. Fortified by these examples, we take courage, and no longer hide under the pillow the works of Poe, Wilkie Collins, Dickens, Doyle, or even Fletcher, when Aunt Emma comes into the room.

A year or more ago a writer of reviews announced with finality that the crime wave in literature was past; that publishers had ceased to publish works about murder; the fad was over; the craze finished. I am glad that he was a false prophet, both because he has been able to write more of his interesting reviews, and that he may be encouraged to write another of his own books about law breakers.

It is true that in the large number of volumes on crime there have been many that ranged from trivial to worthless. But no such phrase could be applied to the scholarly work which characterizes this series of Notable Trials; nor to the notable achievement in the volumes of essays by H. B. Irving, William Roughead, Sir John Hall, Miss Tennyson Jesse, William Bolitho, and the newcomer, Frederick Mackenzie.

If one seeks for a better excuse than mere entertainment, if the book buyer asks for a solid and serious reason for the Notable Trials in this country, I think it can be found with ease. Here is a history of criminal procedure in the country which has made the most progress in the field. It is offered to the citizens of this country, where criminal justice is a scandal. It is not a record of cruelty and ruthlessness, but of a swift and fairly sure disposition in each case, tempered by mercy when that was indicated.

Thus, an innocent man, Abraham Thornton, even a century ago, was protected by the law against public clamour. A lunatic, Ronald True, was sent where he belonged. A doubtful sentence, on Mrs. Maybrick, was, at any rate, commuted to a lesser penalty; while the deliberate murderers, Neill Cream and G. J. Smith, were promptly obliterated by the hangman instead of being saved alive for release by some foolish executive.

As this last remark will be considered savage by those whose hearts are grieved at the thought that anything whatever should be done to a murderer, no matter how dangerous, it may be useful to say that the modern, enlightened and humane school of criminologists had been permitted to experiment with Neill Cream. He had been once before convicted of a cruel murder, and was given merely a life sentence. This was in Illinois.

While in prison he came into a fortune, by the death of his father, and there was started an agitation for his release so that he might enjoy his money. Nobody opposed the pardon, as far as I know; it is never anybody's business to oppose turning criminals loose again. If anybody does oppose it, he is disposed of by the modern, enlightened and humane school of criminologists: they call him a sadist, and that is good enough argument for them. Everybody who does not believe that murderers should roam the earth at their own sweet will is a "sadist," delighting in torture.

So Neill Cream was released from prison, and he justified the theories of the tender-hearted by going to London and murdering four wretched women— murdering them in a manner which caused them to suffer racking torments before they died.

The Governor of Illinois who pardoned him is still alive, I believe. I have often wondered how he feels about it.

Those who believe in the retention of capital punishment cannot denounce all its opponents as sentimentalists, since there is a strong case against

it. But neither can the opponents of the death penalty say that it does not deter murderers, until we,
in this country, put it into practice. As long as we
execute only four murderers out of 262 (as in New
York in 1923) we cannot say that it does not deter,
for we do not know.

And as long as England and Canada execute
their murderers, and keep the murder rate so low,
it is folly to say that murderers do not fear the
death penalty. The argument about capital punishment is of minor importance compared with the
need of an attitude of mind which seeks to protect
the *future* victims of crime, rather than weep so
much over the fate of convicted murderers.

If the death penalty is abolished, the same folk
who are so sorry for murderers, whose great hearts
throb so violently when a man like the bandit and
murderer Gerald Chapman is put to death, will be
found agitating just as tearfully against the life
sentence. The same sentimental lawyers will make
the same silly appeals to juries, and the same signers
of petitions will be trying to get lifers out of jail
in a few years. They procured the release of Neill
Cream with the result I have described. They have
never ceased to try to get out of prison the child
torturer and murderer, Jesse Pomeroy—the familiar
appeal was made recently, on the ground that
he had "learned Arabic in prison" and would be
a "valuable member of the community."

The project of an American series, similar to the Notable British Trials, does not engage the thought of our publishers. The American State Trials are apparently issued solely as legal works.

But an American series is a fascinating notion. If I could command it, and set the editors at work, what excellent reading there would be in the Trials of the Knapps and Crowninshield for the murder of Captain White of Salem, edited by Arthur Stanwood Pier; the Trial of Albert T. Patrick, edited by Arthur Train; the Trials of Thomas Bram, edited by James B. Connolly; The Trial of John C. Colt, edited by Alexander Woollcott; the Trials of Lieutenant Becker, edited by William Travers Jerome; the Trial of Carlyle Harris, edited by Elinor Wylie; the Trial of Lizzie Andrew Borden, edited by—well, in political language, I am in the hands of my friends.

# THE THREE SISTERS

# CHAPTER XIV

## THE THREE SISTERS

THE story of *The Three Sisters* rests on the authority of a pamphlet, published in 1856, and edited by no less a person than the Rev. O. R. Arthur. If this writer is a trifle abrupt in his statements, it is probably due to his emotions, for he had known the sisters from the cradle, and had but recently come from witnessing their deaths.

Their history was published by Arthur R. Orton, a widely distributed gentleman, since his place of business was Baltimore, Philadelphia, New York, and Buffalo. There is a similarity in the names of O. R. Arthur and Arthur R. Orton which may be significant of something or other.

The Halzingler family came to New York in 1821. They arrived by sea, but we are not told from what land they had sailed. They were three in all: Mr. and Mrs. Halzingler and their son Edmond, who was five. The sisters were not yet born. A slight misfortune happened on the voyage: Mr. Halzingler lost his chest overboard. As it contained his entire fortune, one might have expected them to land at

New York in despair. But not anyone who knew the bulldog breed of the Halzinglers.

The head of the family "merely cast one look at the trunk, regretted that the violent sea prevented his going after it, and then forgot all about it."

Luckily he had $525 in his pocket, and by a successful speculation he turned this into $5,000. He lost some of this in a bank failure, won it back again, and then "in a week removed with his family to Boston." His career in Boston is described by Mr. Arthur in two breathless sentences:

"There, in that renowned city, Mr. Halzingler increased his fortune to two hundred thousand dollars. Then, resolving to retire from active life, he removed with his family to Arkansas."

Like Napoleon, Mr. Halzingler made his strokes with the sudden pounce of an eagle. As far as his biographer tells us, his progress from New York to Arkansas was in two leaps; one to Boston, where he hardly took off his hat, but merely made two hundred thousand dollars; then one more jump to Little Rock, Arkansas.

In Little Rock, where he built a "splendid mansion," his three daughters were born. Amy was the eldest, and Elizabeth and Cynthia were twins. Mr. Arthur's style is such as to lead one to suppose that they were all born fifteen minutes after the family arrived in Arkansas, but I suppose that the laws of biology prevailed, even with the Halzingler family.

Mr. Halzingler and his wife were very proud; they "looked down with contempt upon those who possessed not wealth." Moreover, Master Edmond was a bold and fearless rider; at the age of ten he beat a gentleman by the name of Striker in a race; fell off his horse, was taken up senseless, and "four years passed before he was able to leave the house."

His parents thought he would never get up; the doctor differed, and said that he would recover. Whereupon, they instantly presented the doctor with a check for $5,000. That was the way they did things.

"The doctor bowed his thanks, entered his carriage and drove off."

Probably he lashed his horses to the bank, before Mr. Halzingler should change his mind about the check.

Meantime, the three sisters were a cause of great anxiety: disobedient, impudent, and resisting all attempts to teach them the rudiments of learning. Mr. Halzingler, in his masterful way, *"dragged"* Amy to a boarding-school kept by one Madame Belmira. It was distant two days' journey, so the process of dragging must have left the girl ruffled.

The girl's father was stern and abrupt with pupil and teacher:

"Come, Amy," said Mr. Halzingler, opening the

carriage-door, "this is the school-house. Will you get out?"

Amy replied by bursting into tears.

"Amy," said her father, sternly, "I do not wish to make a scene here, but, mark my word, if you do not get out immediately, I shall drag you out and give you a good whipping besides."

Amy knowing that her father would keep his word, obeyed. They ascended the stairs to the drawing-room. Madame Belmira was there awaiting their appearance.

"This is my daughter," said Mr. Halzingler to the teacher, a tall, over-dressed female. "You received the note I sent you yesterday, did you not?"

"*Oui, monsieur,*" replied the lady with a bow.

"Your terms suit me, and I, as you see, have brought my daughter here."

"*Oui, mon——*"

"Speak English," said Mr. Halzingler, "I wish my daughter to hear every word you say."

"She is very *petite*—I mean little," said Madame Belmira.

"You will teach her as fast as you can," said Mr. Halzingler, "should she refuse to learn you must whip her."

The lady placed her hand on Amy's head.

"I vill do as you vish, *monsieur,*" she said.

"Your terms are one thousand dollars per

annum," said Mr. Halzingler, "take a little extra care with her, and I will pay you double the sum."

"It shall be done."

"Should I be satisfied with your school," said Mr. Halzingler, "I will, next year, send this young lady's two sisters here."

A few more words passed between them, and then Mr. Halzingler, after bidding his daughter adieu, entered the carriage and drove off.

He had, however, made an evil choice in Madame Belmira. She had been, at the age of sixteen, maid of honour to the unfortunate Marie Antoinette. She attended but little to the morals of her pupils, and this, in the opinion of the reverend author, was due to the fact that while in France, she had been introduced to Voltaire. Two hours' conversation with him made her "look upon death as an eternal sleep." Her influence upon Amy, Elizabeth, and Cynthia was the direct cause of everything which followed—for the two younger daughters soon joined Amy, and all three were under the malign influence of the disciple of Voltaire.

"Years passed on," says Mr. Arthur. With Mr. Halzingler at the helm, the years must simply have zipped by.

"The beauty of the three sisters dazzled every eye. At the school they were called the 'three graces.' They deserved the name, for lovelier girls never saw the sun. They were beautiful in person and feature; but, alas! not in mind. They were well educated, but beauty and education are nothing, without religion accompanies them. We love to gaze upon the rose, we admire its beautiful red, but we dare not pluck it from the parent stem, because we know that every rose conceals a thorn."

They refused to return to attend their mother's funeral until the ceremony was over. When they did arrive, they persisted in playing the piano in defiance of their father's wishes. They learned that Edmond was to inherit three quarters of their father's estate, and that only one quarter was to come to them. So, in collusion with Madame Belmira, and her nephew, Alphonse, a well-known *roué*, recently arrived from Paris, that city of sin, they concocted a fiendish plot.

Alphonse admired Amy, not only as the heiress to $100,000, but for her own sake. His exact words to her were:

"Amy, you are worthy of being the bride of the greatest hell-hound that ever drew breath."

So it was arranged that Alphonse should boast of having seduced Amy under promise of marriage, and thereby provoke Edmond into a challenge. Edmond was then to be killed by Alphonse in a duel —for Alphonse was a dead shot—the girls would get all the money, and everybody live happy ever afterwards.

The scheme fell through. The false news of Amy's

misfortune hastened Mr. Halzingler's death, but not before he found time to tell Edmond that he was bankrupt, so that nobody could benefit by his death, in any event. Alphonse did kill Edmond in the duel, but a stalwart Arkansan, named Travis, thinking the Frenchman's tactics unfair, instantly impaled him with a bowie knife.

When the news reached Madame Belmira (by means of the *Little Rock Gazette*) she went mad.

The three sisters packed their baggage and departed for San Francisco. We know exactly how and when they arrived: on the good ship *Independence*, Captain Balshar, on July 21, 1853. Thus, in a moment, does the Rev. Mr. Arthur give an atmosphere of reality to his narrative.

The girls cut a dash in San Francisco. They took rooms at the best hotel, and the landlord was besieged with requests for an introduction to them. On the night of their arrival, the city was in great excitement about the three beautiful and mysterious girls, who called themselves the Misses Wilson.

It has to be observed that Sister Amy inherited the Halzingler gift of terse speech. Her "Take seats," in the following passage, is worthy of her sire in his most abrupt moments. Here is Mr. Arthur's narrative of the great success of the sisters in their first and only evening in San Francisco:

"Let us take the reader to the Misses Wilsons' room.

"At a small marble-top table were seated the three ladies. We need not tell our readers that their real names were Amy, Elizabeth, and Cynthia Halzingler.

"'Have you put the cards in the drawer?' asked Amy.

"'Yes.'

"'Lay the marked pack on the table," said Amy. 'We may probably have visitors this evening, and we may as well be prepared for them.'

"Hardly had she finished speaking, when the door opened and the landlord entered.

"'I beg your pardon for intruding,' he said, with a low bow, 'but two gentlemen wished me to introduce them to you and——'

"The landlord hesitated.

"'And you could not refuse them,' said Amy. 'Show them in.'

"The landlord went to the door and opened it.

"'Enter,' he said; and our two friends, Moreland and Waffle, entered.

"'This is Mr. Moreland,' said the landlord, 'and this is Mr. Waffle. Gentlemen, the Misses Wilson, from New York.'

"The two gentlemen bowed.

"'We hope we do not intrude,' said Moreland.

"'No, far from it,' replied Amy. 'Take seats.'

"The landlord smiled, and left the room.

"Moreland observed the cards.

"'Ladies,' said he, 'suppose we have a game of cards.'

"'What do you say, sisters?' asked Amy with an almost imperceptible sign.

"'Yes, let us have a game of cards,' replied both.

"'Shall we play for money?' asked Moreland.

"'Yes,' said Amy; 'it will make it the more exciting.'

"The gentlemen drew their chairs up to the table.

"'Wine was formerly the nectar of the gods,' observed Amy.

"Moreland took the hint and rang the bell. When the servant appeared he ordered several bottles of the best wine. In a few minutes it was brought them.

"'And now for a game of cards,' said Amy, drawing out a purse.

"'There are five of us; let the stakes be two thousand each, ten thousand altogether'; and she laid down several bank-notes. 'Take a glass of wine, Mr. Moreland.'

"'Let us increase the stakes to twenty thousand dollars,' said Moreland, on whom the wine was making an impression.

"'Have it as you will,' said Amy, quietly.

"Maddened at their repeated losses, the two men played deeper and deeper. Four bottles of wine were emptied, and they ordered four more.

"At ten o'clock they were losers to the amount of two hundred thousand dollars.

"'What a fool I was to come here at all,' said one of the men.

"'Drink, drink!' exclaimed Amy, filling another glass and handing it to him. 'How like you that? Is not wine a glorious drink! and was not Bacchus a jolly old fellow?'

"'Let this be our last game,' said Moreland, laying his pocket-book on the table. 'There are now two hundred and fifty thousand dollars. If I should lose, to-morrow's sun will rise upon my corpse.'

"Ten minutes passed. Moreland and Waffle rose from the table. The earnings of three years were lost in a single night. Without addressing a word to either of the sisters, they left the room and descended the stairs. In a few minutes they were on their way to the river.

"'Moreland,' said Waffle, as they stood on one of piers, 'I know what you are thinking of. A few struggles and all will be over.'

"'We have wandered over the world hand in hand,' said Moreland; ''tis a pity that such firm friends should be separated by death.'

"'Death shall not separate us,' said Waffle, throwing his arms around his neck. 'Keep a tight hold, Moreland. Now then!'

"One leap and they were in the river. A few

MRS. PAMELA LEE'S INHUMANITY TOWARD MR. LEE

'THE THREE SISTERS.

struggles and the dark waters closed over them forever.

"Let us return to the sisters."

These ladies had other callers and cleaned up precisely half a million before midnight.

"This is glorious!" exclaimed Amy. "Five hundred thousand dollars in a single night! We can leave California to-morrow."

But a Señor Costello (alias Lem Smith), "the greatest gambler in the State" came and insisted on playing. By virtue of his eminence as a gambler he noticed something that had escaped Moreland and Waffle: that the cards were marked. He was so indiscreet as to mention this fact—and what happened to Señor Costello may be seen in the picture.

"What shall we do with the body?" asked Amy.

"Conceal it behind the sofa," replied Elizabeth.

On the morrow they sailed for New York. Crossing the Isthmus they were seized by a band of thieves (called the "Denums") and robbed of their hard-earned money. They were, moreover, subjected to "many insults," and then released and forced into a "weary walk of many miles" to Chagres. Here the inhabitants took pity on the poor wanderers and paid their fare to New York.

So, when they arrived at the Astor House (January, 1854) they would have been perplexed if it had not been for their uncle, Mr. Edmonds, of "Elizabethtown," Arkansas. An appeal to him resulted in an invitation to make his home their own. Innocence was Mr. Edmonds's leading characteristic.

The sisters were unhappy in Elizabethtown. Mr. Edmonds had a family of seven, and two servants. On the arrival of our three heroines he discharged the servants. Amy, Elizabeth, and Cynthia had to do all the work, which was very repellent to them.

One day, having been obliged to work harder than usual, the sisters threw down their things and left the house. They walked toward the wood, and did not address a word to each other until they had reached it. Then throwing themselves upon the grass, Amy spoke:

"'Sisters,' she exclaimed, 'what a strange life is ours. Some years ago we were worth a hundred thousand dollars; last year we were worth a million; to-day we have not a farthing to call our own. Unless something turns up, we are doomed to pass our lives like slaves in the corn-field.'

"'Curses on him!' exclaimed Cynthia, alluding to Mr. Edmonds.

"'Curses are valueless,' said Elizabeth. 'Let us act.'

"'How?' asked Amy and Cynthia together.

"'Our uncle is rich—very rich,' said Elizabeth.

"'Ah, yes, we knew that,' said Amy.

"'If our cousins died, we should be heirs to his property.'

"Amy and Cynthia looked at each other.

"'And if our uncle and aunt were put out of the way,' continued Elizabeth, 'we should be rich once more.'

"'To kill them is easy,' said Amy; 'but how are we to ward off suspicion from us?'

"'Who will suspect three girls like us of so fearful a deed?' replied Elizabeth.

"'Ah, true, true.'

"'We have decided to kill them?'

"'Yes.''

"The sisters then proceeded to make up a plot, the bare mention of which fills us with horror. Their uncle had formerly been a dentist, and in one of his trunks was a bottle of chloroform. To possess this, was the girls' first object. They intended first, to stupefy their victims with the chloroform, and then to murder them. Their diabolical plan, we regret to say it, succeeded."

Armed with the chloroform and three knives, the girls proceeded to exterminate the Edmonds family. Their technique was faultless, but their ill-luck was persistent.

No sooner had the last of the family expired—Mr. Edmonds himself—than six men entered the room.

"'There are the girls who called themselves the Misses Wilson', said one of the men. It was the landlord at whose hotel the sisters boarded while in San

Francisco. 'I arrest you on the charge of murdering Lem Smith, the gambler; also of murdering three persons in that bed, and five young people downstairs.'"

In an hour they were in prison. The law, with its customary brutality, condemned them to be executed, November 30, 1854.

Amy made a long speech on the scaffold. The sheriff more than once intimated that she had said enough, and tried to go on with the execution. But the crowd of Arkansans, who were fascinated by her eloquence, drove him away, and insisted on more oratory.

"The sheriff approached.

"'Your time has expired,' he said.

"'And I have not said all I wish,' said Amy, sadly.

"'Let her speak! Let her speak!' shouted the crowd.

"The sheriff stepped back, and Amy spoke:

"'Friends, life may be likened unto a river. At first it is a little bubbling brook dancing merrily on beneath the shadows of the trees, neither caring nor thinking of the way it is going. Soon it grows larger and larger, increasing in size until it becomes a mighty river, and then with a roaring noise it dashes onward, and at last empties into the ocean. Is not life like that view? The ocean it empties into,

is the ocean of eternity; the roaring noise is con-
science; and when at——'

"'Come, come,' said the sheriff, 'you have
spoken ten minutes past your time, and I can't be
kept waiting here all day.'

"On hearing this brutal speech, the crowd uttered a loud shout, and in spite of all the vigilance
committee could do to prevent them, they pressed
up closely to the scaffold. The sheriff turned pale,
as well he might, for in the hands of many persons
were bowie-knives and revolvers.

"'Seek to interrupt her again, and you'll repent
it!' shouted several persons.

"The sheriff again stepped back."

Amy—whose admirable brevity had quite deserted her—now delivered a sermon which lasted
three quarters of an hour. At its end, the sheriff
was allowed to terminate the proceedings.

"Reader!" exclaims the reverend author, "shall
we not learn a lesson which shall last us while we
live, from the fate of the Three Sisters? Is not their
experience a warning to our fathers, mothers,
sisters, brothers, and to us? Let us at all times be as
truly repentant as were the Three Sisters upon the
scaffold. Let us hope that they are now in Heaven!"

# A YANKEE CASANOVA

# CHAPTER XV

ALONG the roads and lanes of New England and New York there used to wander a tall fellow with a merry eye and affable manner. Sometimes he went mounted, but often a-foot, and his business, he might tell you, was that of an "Indian doctor."

With "yarbs" and decoctions, he would try to cure any disease. Some of his patients actually got well.

His name, he would say, if this happened to be one of the places where it was safe to use his real one, was Henry Tufts. I think that he and his neighbours sometimes pronounced the last name as if it were "Turf."

He might not be a doctor when you met him. One winter he travelled about with a "peep-show" on his back. This was a far-off, feeble ancestor of the moving-picture theatre: a contrivance for exhibiting pictures in a black box. It once formed an important feature of wayfaring life in America, and has now completely vanished.

The pictures were not naughty ones (as our suspicious generation is ready to imagine), but coloured views of foreign scenes and historic events. Not that Henry Tufts would have been at all reluctant to exhibit the improper kind, if he could have found them.

Tufts might be wandering from place to place neither healing the sick nor showing pictures, but always with some glib explanation of what he was doing. If you showed much curiosity, or looked as if you might be a constable or deputy sheriff, or if you asked any questions about his horse, and where he got such a fine one, Tufts would say that he had to pay a visit; he would turn up the next lane and ride off, leaving you alone.

To whatever profession he might pretend, Tufts had one calling which occupied him for thirty years. First and foremost, he was a thief. In many towns and villages of New Hampshire, Massachusetts, and Vermont he was as welcome as the smallpox. He would burglarize a shop, or steal turkeys from a farmer. He raised the theft of horses almost to the rank of a science: stealing a horse in one town, selling him in another, and then stealing him again for another sale.

The townspeople did well to be careful of their wives, daughters, and maidservants when this robber was about; for he was a thief of virtue, a devil with the women, if his scandalous boastings were true.

This was in the years before, during, and immediately after the American Revolution, when the country roads had a fair supply of wandering rascals. Few of them were so notorious or so amusing as this fellow, whose mortal parts have been in the grave for almost a century, while his soul—unless the clergy of his day were grievously mistaken—has been undergoing especial and exquisite torment.

For, in addition to breaking all of the commandments, except (so far as we know) the one against murder, he added disrespect for religion, and one or two other sins, which even the most complacent person would call pretty black.

He betrayed the faith of man and woman, and possessed not even that honour which some trusting people believe to exist among thieves. Long after his disreputable old age had come to an end, his name was as a hissing and a by-word in the region where he was born and died. Within the memory of people recently living, it was an accepted simile to say that this man, or that, was "as big a thief" or "as bad a liar as old Hen Turf."

The chief source of information about this ancient is a book called *A Narrative of the Life, Adventures, Travels and Sufferings of Henry Tufts*. It is told throughout in the first person, but it is really the work of what we now call a "ghost writer." This appears from the title page, which says, clearly enough, that the book is "In substance, as compiled from his own mouth."

Only one edition is known, and copies of this are so rare that one or two persons, specialists in early Americana, to whom I made inquiry, were inclined to think the book non-existent, or to dismiss it as a chap-book or pamphlet.*

It is, however, a veritable book of more than three hundred pages, and it was printed and published in Dover, New Hampshire, in 1807.

Probably some of the horrified townsfolk thought that the Divine wrath was exhibited in a manner singularly wholesome, when the office of the printer was burned down, and when, not long after, the printer himself succumbed to disease and melancholia.

Others may have held that the Heavenly Censor took a long time to come to a decision, since it was four years after publication of the book before the blow fell upon the printer and his press.

A considerable stock of books, by the way, was burned at the time, and this may account, in part, for the rarity of Henry Tufts's narrative. The book was not one to be bought and preserved by libraries

---

*Colonel, the Reverend Thomas Wentworth Higginson was one of the first discoverers of Henry Tufts, in our time. He read the copy in the Worcester Public Library, now in the American Antiquarian Society Library, and wrote "A New England Vagabond" in his book "Travellers and Outlaws" (1889). This is also in Harper's Magazine, March, 1888. Tufts' book is owned by some other public and private collections, but is missing from many important libraries.

at that time, because of the theory that chronicles of rascality are disreputable, unless the rascality is antique. If some graceless member of a family obtained a copy, there were, doubtless, others in the household, scandalized elders or righteous juniors, who would kindle a private bonfire of purification. For whatever reasons it may have vanished, you will have to be at some pains to see the book.

Tufts was born—so he says—in Newmarket, New Hampshire, in 1748. He is not infallible with his dates. He claimed respectable ancestors, and plumed himself upon a grandfather, Thomas Tufts, who "finished his education at the university of Cambridge"—he means Harvard College—and was afterwards a minister in Boston, until his death in 1725.

As with nearly all of Henry Tufts's statements, there are discrepancies here, which do not disprove the general truth of his narrative. There were two graduates of Harvard at this period, named Thomas Tufts, and the one who took his bachelor's degree in 1701 and died in 1733 seems to have had the best chance of being the author's grandfather. He also had the good fortune to die before his grandson's rise to infamy.

Henry Tufts always felt that he had ancestral claims upon Harvard, and on one perilous occasion made use of this belief.

His parents were respectable; he lays no blame upon influences of heredity.

"My infantile years," he writes, "exhibited none of those characteristic marks of a depraved disposition which were so fully developed in my riper manhood. . . . The following account is little other than a detail of the crimes I have committed and of the frauds and impositions I have practiced upon others."

He showed no originality as a boy: he stole apples, pears, cucumbers, and "other fruits" from the neighbours. He stole a paper money bill from a woman; was made to confess the sin; and was in disgrace in the village. The theft of a sickle was more profitable, for after hiding it for a time, he was able to sell it.

At the age of twenty-one he applied to his father for his share of the estate, which was valued at $1,000. His father declined, saying that the estate was going to Henry's elder brother. The young man felt that this gave him a grievance; he had received no education, and no means of earning except by labour. To work on a farm or anywhere else was distasteful, so he stole his father's horse and sold him in Chester for $30.

With this money he wandered about for two months, leading a very congenial life. At last, however, he went home; gave his father what remained of the money, and received his forgiveness. It was the first of the many acts of forgiveness which were extended to Henry Tufts, constantly encouraging him to go on with his career.

He records his minor pranks with much satisfaction: how, on two different occasions, he stole a beehive. How, on a "pedestrian expedition" through Vermont, he carried with him the small claw of a lobster, which he told people was "an enchanted horn" enabling him to predict future events. He added that he had once had another and larger horn, which made it possible for him to "foretell past events," and said that this greatly impressed the natives, but how it benefited him he does not relate.

Characteristic of his times is a piece of cruelty which he practised upon Deacon Tash of Newmarket, whom he was helping to load a wagon with hay. Tufts had concealed a nest of wasps, which he tossed up to the Deacon on the end of his fork. The poor Deacon, working in his shirt, was so violently attacked by the wasps that he fell from the load, and then ran or stumbled into a ditch, where he lay floundering in water and mud.

Tufts was at one time attracted by "a set of religionists stiled new-lights" at Lee, New Hampshire. He learned to imitate their conversation, and appeared as a preacher at Little Falls, Maine, clad in "a new suit of black, a large Scotch plaid gown and cocked up beaver." For a while he imposed on every member of the congregation except a girl named Peggy Cotton, who denounced him for his lewd manner of glancing at her. Peggy was right, but she was unable to convince the others that Tufts was not a saint.

Living in Canterbury, New Hampshire, Tufts constructed a musical instrument, or Pan's pipes, from pumpkin stalks, or, as he calls them, "three pompion vines." He could make, on this, a loud and penetrating note, which carried for a mile. Whether or not for mischievous purposes, he sounded this strange hooter, one still night, from the outskirts of the village, until the air seemed full of unearthly music. The inhabitants were much perturbed, and decided that it was a celestial warning. Straightway there was a revival of religion in Canterbury, and a great improvement in moral behaviour, which lasted for as long as three months.

Here is one of the pleasing incidents of his career as a thief, as he relates it. "Number four," it should be explained, is old Fort Number Four, now Charlestown, New Hampshire. Tufts says:

"Having passed through Number four, I wheeled to the right about; came, in a short time to Nottingham, and soon arrived at Hampton-Falls. Here I wheedled away a large dog, and sold him near Newbury, for ten shillings; but had crossed the Ferry, scarce twenty minutes, when the dog returned to me by swimming. I ventured into a house

SISTER CYNTHIA (AT THE DOOR) "YOU CAN'T COME IN NOW. WE ARE IN CONFERENCE."

THE ARREST OF THE SISTERS

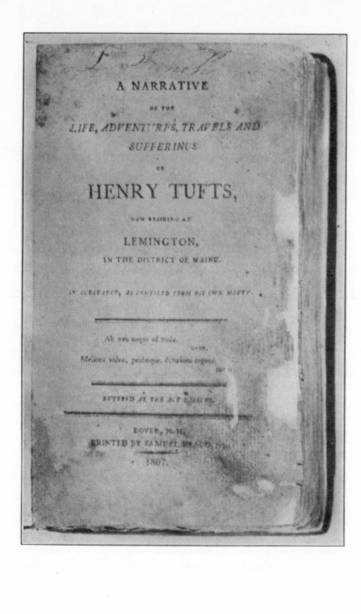

# A NARRATIVE

OF THE

LIFE, ADVENTURES, TRAVELS AND

SUFFERINGS

OF

# HENRY TUFTS,

NOW RESIDING AT

## LEMINGTON,

IN THE DISTRICT OF MAINE.

IN SUBSTANCE, AS COMPILED FROM HIS OWN MOUTH.

Ab ovo usque ad mala.

OVID.

Meliora video, proboque, deteriora sequor.

IDEM.

ENTERED AT THE COPY-RIGHT.

DOVER, N. H.
PRINTED BY SAMUEL BRAGG, JUN.
1807.

in Newburyport, and sold him a second time for six shillings, good money; then taking the road to Bradford, I went on about two miles, when my faithful dog again overtook me. At Bradford I parted with him a third and last time, for about one dollar more; so that, on the whole, my trusty dog turned to a pretty good account. I halted at Bradford just long enough to replenish with food, when my journey was renewed with increased ardor, adopting a sort of disguise, and altering my name, frequently, with a view to baffle pursuit."

His travels carried him into all the New England states except Rhode Island; and often into New York. He made one trip through Pennsylvania and Delaware to Virginia—not greatly to the profit of the people of these states, although the worst that he records of his career in Virginia was one of his raids on a beehive. The sea did not appeal to him, and the longest voyage he mentions was to the Isles of Shoals. He underwent the perils of the deep on this short sail, and vowed to stick to the land.

His favourite jail was in Exeter; he seems to have been confined there eight times; but he was also twice in prison in Maine; often in Dover; in Newbury; and twice in Newburyport. One of his imprisonments in Newburyport was for desertion from the army.

Hurting himself badly with a knife, he suffered a great loss of blood, and his powerful constitution was weakened. It was then that he decided to consult the Indian physicians in Canada. He approached Canada "through the Pigwhacket country" and spent three years with the Indians. He sets down many details of their life. He was not only cured, but mastered their arts of medicine, and became qualified, in his own opinion, to practise them on others.

When he returned to New Hampshire the Revolution had broken out. Reflecting that there might be opportunities for plunder in the army, he served two or three short enlistments each of about three months.* He saw no action, but worked on fortifications and acted as cook. He was stationed at Portsmouth, and at Winter Hill, near Boston. Naturally he was in demand on foraging expeditions—like the soldier in Kipling's "Loot," he often stuffed a gander in his bloomin' haversack.

He declares that he was always honourably discharged, except from his last enlistment, which, unwisely, was for three years. He regretted this and deserted; but suffered no worse penalties than brief imprisonment.

Tufts was a shining example of the habitual criminal, who mocked the law so long as he could cheat and outwit it. When, at last, it really pun-

---

*Here his statements may be checked with other records. Henry Tufts is mentioned as a private soldier on Seavey's Island, Portsmouth Harbour, November 5, 1775, in the *Provincial Papers*, 14:233.

ished him, he radically altered his way of life, and if he did not reform altogether, took a decided turn for the better.

One of the first of his grave crimes was the burglary of a store in Saco. Together with James Dennis, "by nation a Hibernian," Tufts entered by night and robbed the store of a Mr. Pickard, from Ipswich. They stole two large bundles of goods, worth $200.

They carried their loot eight miles away to the house of a fence, one Richard Dutton, and there they remained while Dutton went out to sell the stuff. Dutton aroused suspicion by offering it at too low a price, and was himself arrested. Offering to turn King's evidence, and conduct the sheriff and his men to the hiding place of the thieves, the party arrived at the house at a moment very embarrassing to everyone, for Mr. Tufts was in bed with Mrs. Dutton.

This domestic tangle could not be adjusted, because Tufts and the Hibernian were carried away to Falmouth (now Portland) put in jail, and "confined in irons."

"It was late in autumn [1770]" he writes, "when it was our mishap to become inmates of this horrid mansion, wherefore being destitute of fire and bedding, we suffered miserably during imprisonment."

This was the first time he had ever been in a real prison, and he thought the handcuffs "intolerable." Quite ruthless toward his victims, and usually so toward his fellow thieves, he had the lively self-pity which marks the criminal.

There is no doubt that the Falmouth jail was uncomfortable; and Tufts contrived to make it worse for everyone except himself. He and Dennis tried to burn the building down, and nearly smothered everybody in the smoke.

They were removed to the jail at Old York. Tufts was now celebrated as a malefactor and jail breaker. He was visited by Mr. Pickard, the Ipswich merchant, whom he had robbed. This gentleman made a proposal to the chief robber; nothing is said about the Hibernian, and it is improbable that Tufts bothered about him.

"He said if I would agree to ship with his brother at Newburyport, and sail on a three months' voyage to the West Indies, (he, Mr. Pickard, receiving my wages) that on such condition, he would have me liberated, and, as a further encouragement to behave well, would furnish me with two quintals of fish for a sea venture. To all this I agreed, so Mr. Pickard went and procured my enlargement, by paying, as I supposed, a small matter of cost. We then set out immediately for Ipswich, myself on foot, having no better mode of conveyance. When we had reached Newbury Old Town, he said he had a mind to call in at the next tavern, inviting me to do the like, but I declined. So he told me, if I would behave well, I might continue my journey, and he would overtake me shortly. I said yes, and set forward, but travelling about three quarters of a mile, without company, was so unfortunate as to miss my way, and never came across my deliverer afterwards."

More than twenty years later, and after the close of the Revolution, Tufts had his most disastrous conflict with the law. Of course, he was quite innocent. He was living in Marblehead, Massachusetts with his "wife" and children. The woman was Abigail Kennison, whom he called his "dear Nabby." It is probable that there had been a marriage ceremony; if so, it was fraudulent on his part. At all events, Nabby was his faithful, loving, and long-suffering companion for many years.

Early in 1793, as Tufts relates it, he had bought of one John Stewart, a silver tablespoon and five silver teaspoons. Stewart said he found them in cleaning out a cellar "as he came from Philadelphia." Tufts gave him in return "a fustian coat and a pair of stockings." After all Tufts's plundering, after riding away with droves of horses belonging to other men, it is ironical that he was finally put into jeopardy of his life for six spoons.

A young woman came into his house one day, saw the spoons, and notified the owner of them:

Daniel Jacobs of Danvers. Tufts was arrested and brought before "Esq. Sewall." Stewart was found, and though his statement, as Tufts writes, "was hardly so explicit as I had wished" it almost amounted to a "confession" that he had sold the spoons to Henry Tufts. That cautious statement casts a doubt on Tufts's freedom from at least a guilty knowledge.

Before the trial, Stewart escaped, and Tufts began to dig his way out of the jail. These mining operations were discovered, and the prisoner removed to the jail at Ipswich. This one was strong, and his efforts were now useless. He was brought to trial in June.

In such Massachusetts newspapers for June, 1793, as I have been able to see, I find no account of the proceedings. Tufts's feeble memory for dates may be to blame, or it is possible that the topic was held too trivial to mention. That is entirely possible in the journals of that period. A rather more important capital trial had taken place a few months earlier in Paris, and the American newspapers were still devoting most of their columns to it. This was the condemnation of Louis XVI and its repercussions. Perhaps Henry Tufts was crowded out of the papers by the execution of His Most Christian Majesty.

Tufts applied to Theophilus Parsons, the most eminent lawyer of the county, to defend him. Mr.

Parsons declined, and "Messrs Sewall and Dana" appeared for him.*

The Attorney General, James Sullivan, told Tufts that he was charged with burglary, and that the penalty was death. Tufts was impressed by the fairness of the prosecution. The Attorney General did not argue strongly against him, but warned the jury to be cautious. The Judge charged in his favour.

All that the State's witnesses, Jacobs and the girl, could say was that the spoons belonged to Jacobs, and that on a dark night, when the burglary was committed, they saw a man running from the house. Tufts had no witnesses to prove his property; and he had a bad reputation. In every town in which he lived, as he admits, all robberies were charged to him, and about all that he can say is that not *all* these charges were true.

Three times the jury reported a disagreement: a Mr. Thursten stood out alone for "not guilty." On being sent back a fourth time, they convicted him, and he was sentenced to be hanged on Thursday, August 14, 1793.

Mr. Thursten personally called upon Governor Samuel Adams in behalf of Tufts; and dear Nabby made her piteous appeal. Tufts sent a petition to the "students of Cambridge college" asking them

*Colonel Higginson suggests that these were James Sewall of Marblehead, afterwards a Member of Congress, and Francis Dana, afterwards Chief Justice.

to address the Governor, "and this they had the humanity to do." Tufts adds: "for which they have my sincere thanks." The ladies of Ipswich also made their plea to His Excellency, in pity for the poor convict.

During his dismal wait in jail he was cheered by a visit from a physician. Tufts says that "sunshine sat upon his countenance and honey distilled from his lips ... he presented me with the grief dispelling goblet."

Whether this means that he gave Tufts a drink or read him some optimistic literature does not appear, but he presently spoiled everything by bluntly offering the prisoner two guineas for his skeleton, when he should have no further use for it. Tufts indignantly rejected this nasty proposal.

Next came the publishers: "a gentleman from Newburyport" who offered $70 "for license to publish a narrative of my adventures."

This, also, he declined, on advice from "Esq. Manning" as prejudicial to his chances for a pardon. An anonymous correspondent in Ipswich (perhaps a rival publisher) also advised him to stand firm, and resist all literary temptations.

Finally, the 14th of August arrived. His coffin was made; his grave dug; and the gallows was set up. Three thousand people arrived to witness his death. No reprieve came; but neither did any warrant for the execution. Four o'clock in the afternoon was the hour set: the time came and passed. The three thousand people went away, much disgusted, and Tufts remarks that their departure was witnessed by him with complete resignation.

A month later the sentence was commuted to life imprisonment, and Tufts was removed to the Castle in Boston Harbour. Here he spent five years, and was quite unhappy. He made attempts to escape—once, boldly, by swimming. He compiled a brief dictionary of the language of the underworld, which is printed in his book. He calls it "Nomenclature of the Flash Language" and it may well be the earliest of its kind in America.

Many of its terms also appear in similar dictionaries compiled in England. Thus "cove" means a man; a "flat" is a foolish man; "you're spotted" has the same meaning that it bears to-day; "to do him of his blowen" means to rob him of his wife; and "prad napping" is horse stealing.

His other literary work of his imprisonment was a poem to celebrate the Fourth of July, 1794, beginning:

"Hail! heroes, patriots divine,
On whom the rays of freedom shine."

Years later, on the death of Washington, he wrote ten stanzas of typical verse of the time. No one need put much faith in Tufts's actual authorship of these poems.*

In 1798, Massachusetts ceded the Castle to the United States Government, and the prisoners were transferred. Tufts went to the Salem jail, where he was not desired. The jailer bade him behave himself, with respect to the walls, as they were very weak. This hint was enough to the old escaper, and he was on the road, a free man, in no time at all.

His only problem was whether he should return to dear Nabby or to his lawful wife, Lydia. Nabby was at Greenland, New Hampshire. Lydia, and some of his children, including grown sons, had moved to "Lemington in the District of Maine," where the sons were respected landowners.

He joined his legal family. He was now over fifty years old, and it was suggested to him, by his sons, that they had no insuperable objection if he should try leading a decent life. He agreed; bought some land in Limington,† and set up once more as an Indian doctor. This profession had roving privileges which strongly appealed to him.

He gave a liberal interpretation to his promise to live respectably, but he does seem to have abstained from theft. The terror of the gallows, and

---

*Another notorious convict in Massachusetts, Jesse Pomeroy, does write bad poetry for the prison magazine.

†The present spelling of the name.

the effect of his five years in prison, had gone a long way toward keeping him from crime and only once is he accused of lifting the property of another.

The Shakers, at Alfred, were a community he loved to visit: they were kind and charitable to him, and once, when he was in danger of being cast into Dover jail, on accusation of horse stealing, they rescued him from undeserved imprisonment.

To compare Henry Tufts with that glittering sinner the Chevalier Jacopo Casanova de Seingalt, is strongly deplored by a friend of mine, who says that the New England thief is no more like the brilliant Italian adventurer than a bootlegger's vintage of Scotch whiskey is like the King's Own.

Yet, allowing for the humble state of Colonial society in which Tufts moved, it seems to me that his athletic tendencies, his wandering life, his unblushing recital of his misdeeds, his practice of medicine and magic, his confinement and escape from prisons, his many amorous adventures, and his remarkable versatility constitute enough points of similarity to justify the title of this chapter.

A nearer comparison, perhaps, is with the "Notorious Stephen Burroughs" also of New Hampshire, whose Memoirs were published at Hanover in 1798. Possibly, these suggested the publication of Tufts's book. But, as we have seen, a publisher had approached Tufts as early as 1793.

Tufts is described, on one of his escapes, as

"about six feet high, and forty years of age, wears his own hair, short and dark coloured, had on a long blue coat."

He was a wrestler and boxer and suffered at one time or another five fractures received in wrestling. He once broke a man's arm in a fight, and once wrestled for a stake with a Negro champion, inflicting such injuries that the Negro afterwards died.

Tufts twice received severe floggings, and seems to have borne them without much whimpering. He says that he once offered to take a fellow offender's flogging as well as his own; it is almost the only generous act he claims for himself. On another occasion he betrayed a convict who had planned to escape with him, and not only left the man behind, but stole his clothes, leaving the poor devil naked in his cell.

His love affairs are usually related with the smirk which seems inseparable from such confessions. The language is often heavily classical—as in this.

"I was now free it is true, from the apprehension of a jail, on my forsaken mistress's account, yet not so from the effects of our acquaintance, for the above fascinating amour had made a deep impression on my fancy, and rendered me more unstable than before. Being once initiated into the mysteries of the cyprian Goddess, a natural warmth of

temperament enrolled the name of *Tufts* among
the number of her votaries ever afterwards. In
fine my inclination always fervid, but now fired
with new incentives, impelled me, more strongly
than formerly, to sacrifice at the shrine of Venus,
nor could I resist the impulses of so bewitching a
deity. It was, rather, my coat of arms to pursue
what was pleasing in my own eyes, for to the rigid
graces of self denial I was a stranger. From this
period, therefore, I waxed more industrious in the
pursuit of amorous adventure. . . ."*

His career as a great lover seems to have begun
in Nottingham, New Hampshire. A young lady
named Sally Hall suggested to him a very good
reason why she thought it was desirable for them
to get married. He declined, as he "had not the
most exalted opinion of her virtues and accomplishments."

Next year, when he was twenty-two, he married
Lydia Bickford of Durham. They lived together for
a year or two, and the first of their large family of
children was born. An unfortunate circumstance—
the fact that every theft in the town was imputed
to Tufts—caused the husband to leave his wife
and make his first trip into Maine, in company with
Mr. Dennis of the Hibernian nation. We have seen
how this expedition ended.

---

*This is probably the language of the "clever young lawyer of Dover"
who is the reputed author of the book. His name is not known to me. Another
alleged author is Major or Colonel Thomas Tash of New Durham.

Later, at Claremont, New Hampshire, Enoch Judd, by whom Tufts was employed, suggested that he marry either of his two daughters. The young man agreed, and went with the maiden to Waterbury in Connecticut, where some odd kind of marriage ceremony was performed. Miss Judd, however, soon learned of his other marriage, and of the Saco burglary, so Tufts was again forced into flight.

During his stay in Canada, and as an aid in his studies, Tufts contracted the connection that a high-minded lady once described to her children as a "morganatic" marriage. This was with an Indian damsel, Polly Susap. Her station was regal, since she was "the niece of old King Tumkin Hagen," and she was, moreover, very beautiful. When Tufts deserted her, it was with many promises to return.

His wayside adventures included the conquest of "a young Dutch widow" who kept a tavern somewhere in New York and two girls at Hudson in the same State. The latter lived in a house where Tufts put up for the night: one of them was fair of face and the other very ill-favoured. In the darkness, Tufts made his way, as he thought, to the room of the good-looking one, but found—at the dawning of the day—that he had chosen the other.

He sets down his philosophic reflections to the effect that ignorance is sometimes bliss: and then moralizes, in Dr. Franklin's vein, on the theme that a beautiful countenance is not the first requisite in wife or mistress.

On his Southern trip he encountered—apparently somewhere in Pennsylvania—"a young woman of German extraction" who was riding along the highway, and ready to converse with an agreeable young man. She was a widow, and frankly confessed that she was looking for another husband, and manager of her plantation. Tufts was received by the lady's father as prospective son-in-law and heir. He settled down as overseer of the slaves.

Unluckily, a Lieutenant Mooney came along, and he, says Tufts, "had known me from infancy, egg and bird." So Pennsylvania lost Henry Tufts.

The affair with Abigail Kennison, his dear Nabby, began at Greenland, New Hampshire. He presented himself to her under the pleasing name of Gideon Garland. Subsequently Abigail "swore her child on him," and Tufts was arrested on charge of bastardy. He managed to defraud everybody and to escape. Next spring, however, he came back to Nabby and they fled together, with their child.

She was his companion for years, and for a time they lived in Wallingford, Vermont, where he passed as a doctor. After his desertion of her, on his final escape from Salem jail, she returned to Vermont and was there "respectably married."

After Tufts settled at Limington, he resolved to master his "juvenile eccentricities." There did occur incidents to show that, as with Casanova, his philanderings continued beyond middle age. One of these was the encounter with the young religious devotee who wished to borrow a horse. Here is his account of it:

"A certain young woman, of religious deportment, I must conceal her name, called at my house, one day, in the absence of my family, to borrow my horse, to ride a few miles, to a newlight meeting, and for the favour she engaged to pay half a dollar on her return.

"'The horse, young woman,' said I, 'is at your service, only the money must be paid first, for, you know it is ticklish trusting these hard times.'

"She hesitated, since, horse or no horse, half a dollar, prompt payment, was more than she could advance. What then to do, she knew not, for positively, some horse she must have, and none other could be obtained. Her perplexity was obvious, my inflexibility unshaken; she intreated, allured, flattered, but to little purpose; I was as prompt in refusal as she in importunity.

"At length to promote a compromise: I suggested, that payment might be made easy, without the aid of a capital, since I was not absolutely disinclined to take personal services, in lieu of all other requital. In fine I named the conditions that should, alone entitle her to the loan of the horse, though for modesty's sake, I choose not to repeat them here.

"This was enough to excite those blushes, which I then saw redden on her cheek; I, too, was prepared for the mortification of a rebuff; but the young religionist, after a little hesitation, and a few female negatives, which often carry a far different meaning, gesticulated her assent. Articles of agreement having been fulfilled to a punctilio, she mounted her steed with agility, and rode away with the air and gravity of a vestal of three score."

At another time, during this period, while following the career of a wandering doctor, he mentions "a brisk young widow at Old Wells." His courtship of her "equalled in duration Jonah's continuance in the whale's belly, that is, three days and nights."

His final escapade was forced upon him. He had restored to health, after long illness, a farmer's daughter, a girl of eighteen. As a mark of gratitude she insisted on eloping with him, and they journeyed together on horseback, still farther into Maine.

It was disastrous for Tufts. The girl proved a wanton jade, and treated her companion to one humiliation after another. Of course, Tufts was highly indignant; he could not have been vexed when the girl's father overtook them, and dragged her back to her own place.

Tufts returned to Lydia, to Limington, and to respectability. Nobody can think that it was a drab and stodgy respectability. He was actually reformed—that is, he died—on January 31, 1831, in what Colonel Higginson called "the eighty-third year of an uncommonly misspent life."

The discrepancies in names and dates, throughout the book, are not fatal to a belief that his story is substantially true. It has both embroideries and suppressions, but these occur in the biographies of far more honest men.

**THE END**